Charles Abel Heurtley

A History of the Earlier Formularies of Faith

of the Western and Eastern Churches - to which is added an exposition of the

Athanasian Creed, being the substance of a course of lectures

Charles Abel Heurtley

A History of the Earlier Formularies of Faith
of the Western and Eastern Churches - to which is added an exposition of the Athanasian Creed, being the substance of a course of lectures

ISBN/EAN: 9783337361129

Printed in Europe, USA, Canada, Australia, Japan

Cover: Foto ©Lupo / pixelio.de

More available books at **www.hansebooks.com**

A HISTORY
OF THE
EARLIER FORMULARIES OF FAITH
OF THE
WESTERN AND EASTERN CHURCHES:

TO WHICH IS ADDED

An Exposition of the Athanasian Creed;

BEING

THE SUBSTANCE OF A COURSE OF LECTURES

BY

THE REV. CHARLES A. HEURTLEY, D.D.,
THE LADY MARGARET'S PROFESSOR OF DIVINITY,
AND CANON OF CHRIST CHURCH, OXFORD.

James Parker and Co.
6 SOUTHAMPTON-STREET, STRAND, LONDON;
AND 27 BROAD-STREET, OXFORD.

1892.

PRINTED BY JAMES PARKER AND CO.,
CROWN YARD, OXFORD.

ADVERTISEMENT.

The following pages are intended to be a Companion Volume to the Author's Compilation DE FIDE ET SYMBOLO, so far as regards the Formularies of Faith contained in the last mentioned. They comprise the substance of a Course of Lectures of which those Formularies were the basis.

ST. MATTHEW xxviii. 19.

"Go ye and teach all nations, baptising them IN THE NAME OF THE FATHER, AND OF THE SON, AND OF THE HOLY GHOST."

CONTENTS.

CHAPTER I.

	PAGE
THE CREEDS IN GENERAL	3

CHAPTER II.

CREEDS OF THE WESTERN CHURCH . . .	19
i. Declarative Creeds	*ib.*
ii. Probable dates of additions or alterations in the several Articles . .	32
iii. Interrogative Creeds	37
The Apostles' and Nicene Creeds Harmonized	42

CHAPTER III.

CREEDS OF THE EASTERN CHURCH . . .	49
i. Declarative Creeds	*ib.*
ii. Interrogative Creeds	95

CHAPTER IV.

THE DEFINITION OF FAITH OF THE COUNCIL OF CHALCEDON AND THE QUICUNQUE VULT, COMMONLY CALLED THE ATHANASIAN CREED . .	103
i. The Definition of Faith of the Council of Chalcedon	*ib.*
ii. The Quicunque Vult, commonly called the Athanasian Creed . . .	115

	PAGE
APPENDIX I. The Quicunque and the Treves MS. compared	135
APPENDIX II. Parallelisms between the language of the Quicunque and that of the Commonitory of Vincentius of Lerins	138

CHAPTER V.

AN EXPOSITION OF THE QUICUNQUE VULT, COMMONLY CALLED THE ATHANASIAN CREED	143
INDEX	163

CHAPTER I.
THE CREEDS IN GENERAL.

S. Cyrill. Hieros. Catech. v. § 12.

ΠΙΣΤΙΝ δὲ ἐν μαθήσει καὶ ἐπαγγελίᾳ κτῆσαι καὶ τήρησον μόνην τὴν ὑπὸ τῆς Ἐκκλησίας νυνί σοι παραδιδομένην, τὴν ἐκ πάσης γραφῆς ὠχυρωμένην. . . . Οὐ γὰρ ὡς ἔδοξεν ἀνθρώποις συνετέθη τὰ τῆς Πίστεως, ἀλλ' ἐκ πάσης γραφῆς τὰ καιριώτατα συλλεχθέντα μίαν ἀναπληροῖ τὴν τῆς Πίστεως διδασκαλίαν. Καὶ ὅνπερ τρόπον ὁ τοῦ σινάπεως σπόρος ἐν μικρῷ κόκκῳ πολλοὺς περιέχει τοὺς κλάδους, οὕτω καὶ ἡ Πίστις αὕτη ἐν ὀλίγοις ῥήμασι πᾶσαν τὴν ἐν τῇ παλαιᾷ καὶ καινῇ τῆς εὐσεβείας γνῶσιν ἐγκεκόλπισται.

CHAPTER I.

THE CREEDS IN GENERAL.

THERE is a tradition mentioned by Rufinus, that, when the Apostles were about to separate, each contributed a several article to a compendium of the chief truths of the Gospel which they had received, and which, in compliance with their Lord's injunction, they were going forth to preach. These articles, when put together, made up what, from this original, was afterwards called "The Symbol[a]."

This tradition obtained a wide currency, at least in the Western Church, after Rufinus's time, and is repeatedly referred to by subsequent writers, as though no doubt were entertained respecting it. Indeed some have gone so far as to assign the several articles, each to its supposed author[b].

---

[a] Rufin. in Symb. § 2. The tradition is accepted by the Church of Rome, and the clergy are directed to teach it to the people. Catechism. Concil. Trident. De Fide et Symbolo Fidei, I. i. § 3. Erasmus was censured by the University of Paris (Parisienses Theologi) for calling it in question. Vossius, de tribus Symbolis, Diss. i. § 8.

[b] The following, given by M. Nicolas (Le Symbole des Apôtres, p. 43), attributed sometimes to St. Bernard and published among his Works, may serve as an instance:

"Articuli fidei sunt bis sex corde tenendi,
Quos Christi socii docuerunt, pneumate pleni:
Credo Deum Patrem, Petrus inquit, cuncta creantem,
Andreas dixit, Ego credo Jesum fore Christum,

Nothing however is heard of this tradition before Rufinus's mention of it. St. Cyril of Jerusalem, who wrote some fifty years earlier, and who of all the ancients has left us the fullest commentary on the Creed, has no reference to it. If it had been accepted from the first it is not easy to account for the freedom with which the original document has been dealt with. It would have been handed down, we might have expected, unaltered even to the letter. It has been urged indeed, that, not having been committed to writing but only transmitted orally, variations would naturally creep in. And this might possibly account for the variations, which, setting aside the additions of a later date, are to be found in the Creeds of the Western Church. But it is difficult to understand how the Eastern Church should have felt herself at liberty to depart, so far as she did, from what, on this supposition, was the precise formulary prescribed by the Apostles, and to substitute others in its place, not indeed different in substance but widely different in expression.

Another consideration of great weight is, that St. Cyril of Jerusalem and others of the Fathers do not rest the authority of the Creed on its supposed Apostolic authorship, which they could hardly have

> Conceptum, natum, Jacobus, Passumque Joannes,
> Infera Philippus fugit, Thomasque revixit
> Scandit Bartholomæus, Veniet censere Matthæus,
> Pneuma minor Jacobus, Simon peccata remittit,
> Restituit carnem Judas, Vitamque Matthias."

Unfortunately Art. 9, "sanctam Ecclesiam Catholicam," has been left out.

failed to do had they believed it, but on the ground that its several articles have been gathered out of Holy Scripture, and may be proved thereby [c].

There is however at any rate sufficient uniformity in the ancient Creeds to place it beyond a doubt that, in the main, they sprang from a common origin in the earliest times. Whatever differences there may be in detail, with the sole exception of two later additions in the Western Creed, there is, as to the principal articles, the most entire general agreement. These are substantially the same in all. And it is a striking testimony to the Catholicity of the Church.

[c] Thus Cyrill. Hieros. Catech. v. 12. Καὶ τέως μὲν, ἐπ' αὐτῆς τῆς λέξεως ἀκούων, μνημόνευσον τῆς Πίστεως, ἐκδέχου δὲ, κατὰ τὸν δέοντα καιρὸν, τὴν ἀπὸ τῶν θείων γραφῶν περὶ ἑκάστου τῶν ἐγκειμένων σύστασιν. Οὐ γὰρ ὡς ἔδοξεν ἀνθρώποις συνετέθη τὰ τῆς Πίστεως, ἀλλ' ἐκ πάσης γραφῆς τὰ καιριώτατα συλλεχθέντα μίαν ἀναπληροῖ τὴν τῆς Πίστεως διδασκαλίαν. Euseb. Gall. Homil. i. de Symb., "Ecclesiarum patres, de populorum salute solliciti, ex diversis voluminibus Scripturarum collegerunt verba brevia et certa, expedita sententiis sed diffusa mysteriis, et hoc 'Symbolum' nominaverunt."

The question of the Apostolic origin of the Creed is discussed by Bingham, x. 3. § 5, and by Bull, Judic. Eccles. Cathol. v. 3. Bull is against the Apostolic origin of any definite Formulary. His annotator, Grabe, takes the opposite side. See further, Vossius, de Tribus Symbolis, Ussher, de Symbolo Romano, Suicer, Thesaurus, voc. Σύμβολον, Barrow, and Lord King, in their respective Works on the Creed. M. Nicolas, a recent French writer, holds that till towards the end of the second century the Creed consisted simply of a profession of belief in the three Divine Persons, that afterwards the article on the Church was added, and later still the remaining articles, as the exigencies of the Church required in her maintenance of the truth against the perversions of heresy

I said that the various Creeds must have had a common origin. That origin was without doubt the profession of faith made at Baptism. When any one desired to be admitted into the Church, he would first be instructed in the leading truths of Christianity, and then, when he came to be baptized, would be required to make a formal confession of them. They would necessarily be those which relate to the Father, the Son, and the Holy Ghost, in whose Name baptism was to be administered and to whose service he was to be consecrated, to the birth, death, resurrection, and ascension of Christ, to His future coming to judge the world, to the remission of sins in His Name, and the like. We might seem to have the earliest recorded Creed in the Eunuch's confession, "I believe that Jesus Christ is the Son of God[d]," but unfortunately there is reason to doubt the genuineness of the passage. Some such confession, however, must in all cases have been required and made. And it would naturally be substantially the same in all, however it might vary in the terms in which it was expressed[e].

With regard to the origin of the term "Symbolum," as applied to the Creed, different theories have been held. Rufinus's account, that it was founded on the fact that the Creed was the joint contribution of the Apostles, each having contri-

---

[d] Acts viii. 37.

[e] The following passages may, with more or less probability, be thought to refer to a confession of faith made at baptism. 1 Pet. iii. 21; Rom. x. 9, 10; Heb. x. 22, 23; 1 Cor. xv. 3, 4; 1 Tim. vi. 12; 2 Tim. i. 13; Rom. vi 17.

buted a several article, has been already referred to. Besides this, he suggests others, questionable indeed, but agreeing better with the ordinary meaning of the word: "Either the Formulary was designed to be a sign or token (symbolum) by which true teachers might be distinguished from false, or it corresponded to the watchword given by a General to his soldiers in a civil war, in which the opposing armies spoke the same language and wore the same dress, to enable them to recognise each other, and to distinguish friends from foes. For which reason, he adds, it was forbidden to commit the Creed to writing, lest it should find its way into the hands of unbelievers[f]."

A more probable account of the origin of the name is that it was suggested by the signs or tokens given to those who were admitted to the Heathen mysteries, baptism, previous to the administration of which the Creed was required to be learnt and rehearsed, being the rite of admission to the Christian mysteries[g].

Of the care taken to conceal the Creed from those outside the Church we meet with repeated notices in early writers[h]. Even the Catechumens were not taught it till they were on the eve of baptism. This

[f] Rufin. § 2.

[g] See Vossius, de Tribus Symbolis, Dissert. i. xv. sqq., and Lord King's Critical History of the Creed, pp. 6, &c.

[h] See Cyrill. Hieros. Cat. v. § 12, and August. Sermo ad Catechumm. § 1. Sozomen, e.g. in his account of the Council of Nicæa, says, that he had intended to insert the Creed there agreed upon in his History, but had been dissuaded by his friends, on the ground that it would thus be brought to the knowledge of unbelievers: οἷα δὲ μύσταις καὶ μυσταγωγοῖς μόνοις θεὸν τάδε λέγειν καὶ ἀκούειν. H. E. i. 20.

agrees best with the account last given of the origin of the term "Symbolum." It was the Christian's badge or watchword, the possession of which warranted his participation in the Church's privileges.

It is observable that the word, though of Greek origin, is found for the first time in the works of a Latin Father, St. Cyprian[1]. St. Cyril of Jerusalem, who writes in Greek, does not use it. His term is ἡ πίστις, The Belief. Other names applied to it were Μάθημα, That which the Catechumens have to learn, Κάνων τῆς πίστεως, Κάνων τῆς ἀληθείας, Regula fidei, Regula veritatis, The Rule of the Faith or of the Truth, σύνθεμα, Ἔκθεσις, a Summary or Declaration of Christian Doctrine.

Originally Symbolum Apostolorum or Apostolicum was the designation not of one formulary, as distinguished from others, but of the Creeds generally. It implied that the doctrine set forth, though not necessarily couched in the very words delivered by the Apostles, was at least Apostolic doctrine, such

---

[1] Epist. ad Magnum, and again Epist. ad Episcopos Numidas. "Quæ vox," says the Benedictine Editor of St. Cyril, p. 81, "quanquam Græca sit, prius tamen apud Latinos quam apud Græcos, pro communi fidei confitendæ formula, usurpata reperitur, nec ea ætute qua scribebat hæc Cyrillus satis apud Græcos in usu."

Dr. Swainson, M. Nicolas, and others would distinguish between the terms Symbolum and Regula fidei; but without reason. St. Augustine uses them as synonymous, "Accipite, filii, Regulam fidei quod Symbolum dicitur." Serm. ad Catechumenos, § 1. "Symbolum est breviter complexa Regula Fidei, ut mentem instruat nec oneret memoriam." Serm. 213, § 1.

as the Apostles taught, such as they handed on. They were all in fact looked upon as one and the same in substance, though varying often in the manner of expression[k]. But when distinctive names came to be given to particular Formularies, "Symbolum Nicænum," "Symbolum Constantinopolitanum," then the Western Formulary, which hitherto had had no distinctive name, retained the appellation which had once been common to all, and which thus became itself distinctive.

We are familiar with the Creed as invariably having a place in the public services of the Church: but this was not the case in the earliest times. Its first liturgical use was at Antioch, where it was introduced by Peter Fullo, A.D. 471 [1]; its next at Alexandria, some seven years later, its next at Constantinople, A.D. 511 [m]. Our first notice of it in connexion with the Western Offices is, that the 3rd Council of Toledo, A.D. 589, at the suggestion of

[k] In the Mozarabic Breviary, e.g., the Constantinopolitan Creed is styled "Symbolum Apostolicum," col. 945.

[1] Theodorus Lector, lib. ii. p. 566, Vales., ἐν πάσῃ συνάξει.

[m] Ibid. p. 563. At Constantinople it had been recited previously only once a year, namely, on the Thursday in Holy Week, ἐν τῇ ἁγίᾳ παρασκευῇ τοῦ Θείου πάθους, τῷ καιρῷ τῶν γενομένων ὑπὸ τοῦ ἐπισκόπου κατηχήσεων. The Creed specified is that of "the 318," though by that title the Creed of Constantinople was probably intended (see Voss. de Tribus Symbolis, III. 4, 5), the object, ἐπὶ διαβολῇ δῆθεν Μακεδονίου, ὡς αὐτοῦ μὴ δεχομένου τὸ Σύμβολον. Usher, by a strange oversight, seems to have confounded this Macedonius with the earlier Archbishop who gave his name to the Macedonian Heresy. Usher de Rom. Eccles. Symb. Opp. vii. p. 314.

the Gothic King, Recared, ordained that the Creed should be publicly rehearsed in the Liturgy, in all the Churches of Spain and Gallicia, that no man in future might have an excuse for his ignorance, when he was thus made familiar with the Church's belief[n]. At Rome it is said not to have been introduced into the Liturgy till A.D. 1014, after which time its liturgical use became general throughout the West. This, however, requires modification. Mabillon adduces proofs of an earlier use, only with this difference, that in that earlier use the Creed was simply rehearsed. From and after 1014 it was chanted.

These remarks, however, must be understood of the Nicene, or rather the Constantinopolitan Creed, which from the first was commonly called the Nicene (see note y, p. 15, below). As regards the Apostles' Creed, this was used in the Breviary of the Western Church, its place being after the Lord's Prayer, at Prime. It occurs commonly in ancient Psalters among the Hymns of the Church, the *Te Deum*, &c., at the end. Some of these Psalters are probably as old as the eighth century. But of the time when it was first admitted, we have, so far as

---

[n] De Aguirre, Collect. Concill. Tolet. III. xxvii. Pro reverentia sanctissimæ fidei, et propter corroborandas hominum invalidas mentes, consultu piissimi Domini nostri Recaredi, sancta constituit synodus, ut per omnes ecclesias Hispaniæ vel Gallæciæ, secundum formam Orientalium Ecclesiarum, Concilii Constantinopolitani, i.e. CL. Episcoporum, Symbolum Fidei recitetur, quo et fides vera manifestum testimonium habeat, et ad Christi Corpus et sanguinem prælibandum, pectora populorum, fide purificata, accedant.

I can find, no record º. Certainly it had no place in the Church's service in Africa in St. Augustine's time ᵖ. In Spain it was not introduced till the eleventh century, when the Roman use after long and strenuous opposition was substituted for the Mozarabic ᵠ.

Our Reformers retained both Creeds when they reconstructed the English Offices, and with wise discretion. The one finds an appropriate place in the daily morning and evening services, the other suitably precedes the celebration of the Christian Mysteries in the Communion Office, to which none but the faithful have a right to be admitted.

But though in the earlier ages the Creed formed no part of the Church's ordinary service, yet great pains were taken to teach it and explain it to the candidates for baptism. Several of the early Expositions which have come down to us are expository addresses which were delivered to Catechumens with

---

º Mr. Ffoulkes, in a Letter to the "Times," Feb. 17, 1873, says, speaking of the ancient MS. Psalters, "The pieces which follow the Psalter were added in general as they became popular, or were taken into the Service, or both. The Lord's Prayer is ordered to be said at Prime with the Psalter, in the Regula Canonicorum of Chrodegund, Bishop of Metz, the Apostles' Creed is not. In a Vatican MS. of the Synod of Aix, A.D. 816, that is about fifty years later, the use of this Creed is enjoined; and Amalarius, Presbyter of Metz of that date, testifies in his Work, de Eccles. Off., to its being in use in his time, after the Lord's Prayer. The Athanasian Creed was ordered to be used on Sundays at Prime, shortly afterwards."

ᵖ See St. August. Serm. 58, § 13, Opera, tom. v. Paris, 1837.

ᵠ Nicolas, p. 267.

the latter object in view, St. Cyril's, for instance, and most of those in St. Augustine's Works. These addresses are generally entitled "Sermones in Traditione Symboli," or "In Redditione Symboli."

The "Traditio Symboli" was the oral delivery of the Creed to the Catechumens that they might learn it by heart[r]. This was ordinarily done on a stated day, in some Churches, as the French, Spanish, and Milanese, on Palm-Sunday; in others, at Rome for instance, on the Fourth Sunday in Lent, Easter-Eve being the great day appointed for the Celebration of Baptism[s].

The "Redditio Symboli" was the rehearsal of the Creed when learnt, by the Catechumens, before the Bishop and Presbyters in the Church, and for this also a certain day was prescribed, the Parasceue, or day before our Lord's Passion. And this was the only day, for some ages, on which the Creed was publicly recited in the Church[t]. It was again re-

---

[r] See Martene, de Antiquis Ecclesiæ Ritibus, l. 1. c. 1. art. xi. In some instances, even in the Western Church, the Constantinopolitan Creed was thus delivered. Sometimes the Creed was delivered in both Greek and Latin, as in the Gelasian Sacramentary. See other instances mentioned by Martene, vol. i. p. 85, § 16. The Creed is usually preceded by a short preface, and followed by a short Exposition.

[s] The principal times of Baptism were Easter and Whitsuntide, and, though not to so great extent, the Epiphany. Bingham, xi. 6, 7.

[t] This was the day fixed by the Council of Laodicea, Can. 46. But it appears that in some Churches other days were customary, as, at Rome, the morning of the Sabbatum Sanctum, Easter Eve. Martene, vol. i. p. 85, and p. 116, § 11.

peated by the Catechumens at their baptism; but in this case not continuously, but in answer to the interrogatories then put, often in a shortened form, of which many examples are found in Baptismal Creeds still extant in ancient Sacramentaries[u].

I have already hinted that there are two distinct classes of Creeds, the Western and the Eastern. A comparison between them will justify me in making the distinction. The Apostles' Creed, as we term it, may stand as the representative of the one class, the Nicene (Constantinopolitan) of the other. To describe broadly the difference, the Western are more simple than the Eastern, the reason of which would seem to be that the West was less troubled with heresy in the earlier ages than the East. And to this in part Rufinus ascribes it that the Church of Rome had preserved the simplicity of its original text

---

[u] See the author's Harmonia Symbolica, where several Interrogative Baptismal Creeds are given. One of these follows at the end of this note, some others below, chap. II. iii.

In the Gelasian Sacramentary the Creed occurs three several times in the services connected with Baptism. First, on the Saturday before Palm Sunday we have the Traditio Symboli, the recitation of the Constantinopolitan Creed, first in Greek, then in Latin, followed by a short Exposition. (Muratori, col. 540.) Then, on the morning of the following Saturday, Easter Eve, the Redditio Symboli (col. 563). In the evening of the same day the Baptism is administered, the Catechumens, or the sponsors in their names, having been first questioned as to their faith in three interrogatories: 1. Credis in Deum Patrem omnipotentem? *Resp.* Credo. 2. Credis et in Jesum Christum, Filium ejus unicum, natum et passum? *Resp.* Credo. 3. Credis et in Spiritum Sanctum, Sanctam Ecclesiam, Remissionem peccatorum, Carnis Resurrectionem? *Resp.* Credo.

unaltered, another cause being the custom already referred to which prevailed there, of requiring the candidates for baptism to rehearse the Creed publicly in the bearing of the congregation. "In some Churches," he says, "additions have been made to the first article. Not so, however, in the Church of Rome, the reason of which I conceive to be, on the one hand, that no heresy has originated there, on the other, that the ancient custom is still observed of requiring those who are about to be baptized to rehearse the Creed publicly in the audience of the faithful; the consequence of which is that the addition of even a single word would at once be detected and disallowed [x]."

It may sound strangely perhaps to some that I should speak of various Creeds, as though implying that there are many, seeing that they are familiar with but three, and are accustomed to hear them spoken of as "*the* three Creeds," as though these were all that are known, or, at any rate, all that are recognized. And in truth these are all, for the most part, that, so far as use is concerned, have survived to this day. But there are still extant a considerable number of Creeds which were in use in the ancient Church, one in one of its branches, another in another. These, however, were not, in strictness, different Creeds but rather varieties of the one Confession which the Church Catholic has professed from the beginning. The truth is, that for some centuries each Church seems to have felt itself at liberty to use its own

[x] Rufin. in Symb. § 3. See St. Augustine's interesting account of the baptism of Victorinus. Confess. viii. § 2.

Formulary, and even to make additions or alterations provided that it did not in substance depart from the faith once for all delivered to the Saints. Hence arose variations in detail in the midst of substantial oneness and harmony. "In veste varietas non scissura"—The garment might be of diverse colours, but it had no rent.

In the East the Creeds of particular Churches gradually gave way before the Creed of Constantinople, which is what we now call, and has from very early times been called, the Nicene Creed, as being, in fact, simply an enlarged edition of the Nicene Creed strictly so called [y]. The Western Churches, while accepting and using the Constantinopolitan Formulary, still retained their own Creeds, each at first with its own peculiarities, but eventually all agreeing in the text which, through successive centuries, has come down to the present day.

[y] Suicer, De Symbolo Nicæno-Constantinopolitano, p. 14. Vossius, De Tribus Symbolis, Diss. iii. Theses 4 and 5. Epiphanius when recording a Creed, which is as nearly as possible identical with that which was adopted at Constantinople some seven years afterwards, calls it "the Creed set forth in the holy city by all the holy bishops there assembled, more than 310 in number," evidently meaning the Nicene Council, as though the Creed which he quotes is to all intents and purposes identical with the Nicene. The Council of Chalcedon, in their Definition of Faith, virtually identify the Constantinopolitan with the Nicene, the one being simply an enlarged edition of the other, enlarged to meet the requirements of heresy. Οὐχ' ὥς τι λεῖπον, they say, τοῖς προλαβοῦσιν ἐπάγοντες, ἀλλὰ τὴν περὶ τοῦ Ἁγίου Πνεύματος αὐτῶν ἔννοιαν κατὰ τῶν τὴν αὐτοῦ δεσποτείαν ἀθετεῖν πειρωμένων γραφικαῖς μαρτυρίαις τρανέσαντες. Def. Fidei Concil. Chalced.

The Western Creed would seem to have reached its complete form in the first instance in France, and to have owed its wide circulation and general adoption, as Dr. Swainson suggests, to the Psalters which were written in great numbers by French scribes, in the reign and by the encouragement of Charlemagne[z].

[z] The Nicene and Apostles' Creeds, p. 170.

CHAPTER II.

CREEDS OF THE WESTERN CHURCH.

S. August. de Trinitate xv. § 51.

Domine Deus noster, credimus in Te, Patrem, et Filium, et Spiritum Sanctum. Neque enim diceret Veritas, 'Ite, baptizate omnes gentes in Nomine Patris et Filii et Spiritus Sancti,' nisi Trinitas esses. Nec baptizari nos juberes, Domine Deus, in Ejus Nomine qui non est Dominus Deus. Neque diceretur voce divina, 'Audi Israel, Dominus Deus tuus Deus unus est,' nisi Trinitas ita esses, ut unus Dominus Deus esses.

CHAPTER II.

CREEDS OF THE WESTERN CHURCH.

I. DECLARATIVE CREEDS.

1. LYONS (ST. IRENÆUS), *circ.* A.D. 175—185.

THE earliest document which has come down to us, at all approaching to a formal Creed, whether of the Eastern or the Western Church, if we except the short Creed from St. Cyril of Jerusalem, given below, is contained in the first book of St. Irenæus's great work against Heresies, the date of which, according to Bishop Lightfoot, must be placed soon after A.D. 175[a]. St. Irenæus serves as a link to connect the East and West together. By birth and education he belonged to Asia Minor, where in his youth he had been a hearer of Polycarp, whom one or more of the Apostles had set over the Church of Smyrna. Afterwards he settled at Lyons, and on the martyr-death of Pothinus its bishop, A.D. 177, succeeded to the see of that city.

Irenæus's Creed is rather a paraphrase than a transcript of the exact words of the Formulary actually in use: but it shews sufficiently what that Formulary

---

[a] St. Ignat. i. p. 381. It was written, as Irenæus himself says, while Eleutherus was Bishop of Rome, i.e. between 170 and 185. Irenæus must have been born in the first quarter of the second century.

must have been. In its type it is Eastern: nor is this surprising, the south-eastern district of Gaul having apparently derived its Christianity directly from the East. Not only its Creed but its earliest Liturgy also bears traces of an eastern origin.

St. Irenæus's work contains three notices of the Creed with which he was familiar. In introducing the one which would seem to come nearest to the exact Formulary, he speaks of it as "the Rule of Truth," κάνων τῆς ἀληθείας, which the orthodox Christian had received at baptism and still kept. In form it was framed, as I said just now, on the eastern model, in substance it was the one faith believed and professed throughout the whole Church.

"For the Church," he says, "though dispersed throughout the whole world, has been taught by the Apostles and their disciples to believe

1. εἰς ἕνα Θεὸν Πατέρα παντοκράτορα,
   τὸν πεποιηκότα τὸν οὐρανὸν καὶ τὴν γῆν,
   καὶ τὰς θαλάσσας, καὶ πάντα τὰ ἐν αὐτοῖς·
2. Καὶ εἰς ἕνα Χριστὸν Ἰησοῦν, τὸν Υἱὸν τοῦ Θεοῦ,
3. Τὸν σαρκωθέντα ὑπὲρ τῆς ἡμετέρας σωτηρίας·
8. Καὶ εἰς Πνεῦμα ἅγιον,
   τὸ διὰ τῶν προφητῶν κεκηρυχὸς τὰς οἰκονομίας, καὶ τὰς ἐλεύσεις,
(3) καὶ τὴν ἐκ Παρθένου γέννησιν,
(4) καὶ τὸ πάθος,
(5) καὶ τὴν ἔγερσιν ἐκ νεκρῶν,
(6) καὶ τὴν ἔνσαρκον εἰς τοὺς οὐρανοὺς ἀνάληψιν τοῦ ἠγαπημένου Χριστοῦ Ἰησοῦ, τοῦ Κυρίου ἡμῶν,
(7) καὶ τὴν ἐκ τῶν οὐρανῶν ἐν τῇ δόξῃ τοῦ Πατρὸς παρουσίαν αὐτοῦ

ἐπὶ τὸ ἀνακεφαλαιώσασθαι τὰ πάντα,

(11) καὶ ἀναστῆσαι πᾶσαν σάρκα πάσης ἀνθρωπότητος,
ἵνα Χριστῷ Ἰησοῦ, τῷ Κυρίῳ ἡμῶν, καὶ Θεῷ, καὶ
Σωτῆρι, καὶ βασιλεῖ, κατὰ τὴν εὐδοκίαν τοῦ Πατρὸς
τοῦ ἀοράτου, πᾶν γόνυ κάμψῃ ἐπουρανίων καὶ ἐπι-
γείων καὶ καταχθονίων, καὶ πᾶσα γλῶσσα ἐξομο-
λογήσηται αὐτῷ, καὶ κρίσιν δικαίαν ἐν τοῖς πᾶσι
ποιήσηται, τὰ μὲν πνευματικὰ τῆς πονηρίας, καὶ τοὺς
ἀγγέλους παραβεβηκότας καὶ ἐν ἀποστασίᾳ γεγο-
νότας, καὶ τοὺς ἀσεβεῖς, καὶ ἀδίκους, καὶ ἀνόμους,
καὶ βλασφήμους τῶν ἀνθρώπων εἰς τὸ αἰώνιον πῦρ
πέμψῃ, τοῖς δὲ δικαίοις, καὶ ὁσίοις, καὶ τὰς ἐντολὰς
αὐτοῦ τετηρηκόσι καὶ ἐν τῇ ἀγάπῃ αὐτοῦ διαμεμε-
νηκόσι, τοῖς ἀπ' ἀρχῆς τοῖς δὲ ἐκ μετανοίας, ζωὴν
χαρισάμενος, ἀφθαρσίαν δωρήσηται, καὶ δόξαν αἰω-
νίαν περιποιήσῃ.

"This, faith," St. Irenæus continues, "the Church having received, carefully guards, as dwelling in one house, though dispersed, as we said, throughout the whole world; and her belief is in accordance with it, as having one soul and one heart, and her preaching and teaching, and handing on of the tradition are in unison with it, as though she spoke with one mouth. For though the languages of the world are dissimilar, yet in effect, the tradition is one and the same in all. And neither do the Churches in Germany hold another faith, or hand on another tradition, nor those in Spain, nor those in Gaul, nor those in the East, nor those in Egypt, nor those in Libya, nor those in the centre of the earth[b]. But like as

---

[b] Palestine, supposed to be the centre of the earth, τῆς γῆς τὸ μεσώτατον ὁ Γολγοθὰς οὗτος. Cyrill. Hieros. xiii. 28. The

the sun, which is a creature of God, is one and the same throughout the whole world, so also the preaching of the truth shineth everywhere, and enlighteneth all men who desire to come to the knowledge of the truth. And neither will the most eloquent among the Church's prelates say other than this (for no one is above his Teacher), nor will he who is less gifted in aught diminish the tradition. For the faith being one and the same, neither has he, who has much to say concerning it, anything over, nor he who has but little any lack [c]."

II. CARTHAGE (TERTULLIAN), A.D. 186—218.

Tertullian, a Presbyter of Carthage, and a contemporary of St. Irenæus but his junior by some years, has preserved three fragmentary notices of the Creed of his day.

The following from the Treatise de Velandis Virginibus appears to come the nearest to the Normal Formulary [d].

"The Rule of Faith is one and but one, sole, fixed, unalterable, in accordance with which we believe

1. In unicum Deum Omnipotentem,
    Mundi conditorem;
2. Et Filium ejus, Jesum Christum,

belief was founded on a misunderstanding of Ezek. v. 5, "Thus saith the Lord God; This is Jerusalem: I have set her in the midst of the nations, and countries are round about her." On which St. Jerome's comment is, "Jerusalem in medio mundi sitam hic idem Propheta testatur, *umbilicum terræ* eam esse demonstrans." Hieron. *in loc.*

[c] St. Irenæus, contra Hæres. i. c. 2. Ed. Harvey.

[d] De Virginibus Velandis, c. i. p. 173, Paris, 1675.

3. Natum ex Virgine Maria,
4. Crucifixum sub Pontio Pilato,
5. Tertia die resuscitatum a mortuis,
6. Receptum in cœlis,
   Sedentem nunc ad dexteram Patris,
7. Venturum judicare vivos et mortuos,
11. Per carnis etiam resurrectionem."

It will be observed that the 8th, 9th, 10th, and 12th articles are wanting, probably for no other reason than that it did not come within Tertullian's purpose to refer to them. They are supplied, however, by St. Cyprian, a Bishop of the Church of which Tertullian was a Presbyter, but Tertullian's junior by some fifty years.

III. CARTHAGE (ST. CYPRIAN), A.D. 246—258.

St. Cyprian was converted to Christianity, A.D. 246, ordained Presbyter 247, and consecrated Bishop 248. He suffered martyrdom, A.D. 258.

St. Cyprian's notices of the Creed are but fragmentary. The first occurs in an Epistle to one who had consulted him as to whether those who had been baptized by Novatians, who were schismatics but not heretics, might be received into the Church without being rebaptized, St. Cyprian replies, "By no means:" and he proceeds to answer the objections which were urged to the contrary, one of which was that Novatian held the same faith, and used the same form of baptism as the Church:—" Quod si aliquis opponit ut dicat, Eundem Novatianum legem tenere quam Catholica Ecclesia teneat, eodem Symbolo quo et nos baptizare, eundem nosse Deum Patrem, eundem

Filium Christum, eundem Spiritum Sanctum; ac propter hoc usurpare eum potestatem baptizandi posse, quod videatur in interrogatione baptismi a nobis non discrepare, sciat quisquis hoc opponendum putat, primum, non esse unam nobis et schismaticis Symboli legem, neque eandem interrogationem. Nam cum dicunt, ' Credis remissionem peccatorum et vitam æternam per sanctam ecclesiam ?' mentiuntur in interrogatione, quando non habeant Ecclesiam [e]."

We have another fragmentary notice of the Creed in a letter to the Bishops of Numidia, on the invalidity of heretical Baptism [f].

"Sed et ipsa interrogatio quæ fit in Baptismo testis est veritatis, nam cum dicimus, Credis in vitam æternam, et remissionem peccatorum, per sanctam Ecclesiam? intelligimus remissionem peccatorum non nisi in Ecclesia dari."

Putting Tertullian's and St. Cyprian's notices together, we obtain the following as approximately the Creed of Carthage and of the North African Church of the first half of the third century.

IV. CARTHAGE, TERTULLIAN, SUPPLEMENTED BY ST. CYPRIAN, A.D. 200—258.

1. CREDO in unicum Deum Patrem omnipotentem, Mundi Conditorem;
2. Et in Filium ejus Jesum Christum,
3. Natum ex Virgine Maria,
4. Crucifixum sub Pontio Pilato,
5. Tertia die resuscitatum a mortuis,

[e] Ad Magnum, Epist. 69, al. 76.   [f] Epist. 70.

6. Receptum in cœlis,
   Sedentem nunc ad dexteram Patris,
7. Venturum judicare vivos et mortuos;
8. Et in Spiritum Sanctum,
9. Sanctam Ecclesiam,
10. Remissionem peccatorum,
11. Carnis resurrectionem,
12. Vitam æternam.

The "unicum" and "Mundi Conditorem" in Art. 1, were probably Tertullian's own, rather than parts of the Normal Creed of the African Church. The Western Church did not as a rule think it necessary to express the unity in terms, believing it to be implied in the very word "God." For, as Tertullian himself says, "To deny that God is one, is virtually to deny that He is g." As to the "Mundi Conditorem," though the clause, in another form, is almost universal in the Eastern Creeds, we do not meet with it again in the West till the seventh century, and then in the words "Creatorem cœli et terræ."

V. ROME (MARCELLUS OF ANCYRA), A.D. 341.

Hitherto the notices of the Creed which we have met with have been but fragmentary. The earliest complete formulary which has come down to us is a Confession of faith presented by Marcellus, Bishop of Ancyra in Galatia, to Julius, Bishop of Rome.

Marcellus had signalised himself at the Council of Nicæa by his defence of the orthodox faith, and had

---

g Veritas Christiana distincte pronunciavit, Deus, si non unus est, non est; quia dignius credimus non esse quodcunque non ita fuerit ut esse debebit. Adv. Marcion. i. § 3.

drawn upon himself in consequence the hostility of the Arian party, through whose instrumentality he had been anathematised, deposed, and banished as a heretic.

Marcellus repaired to Rome, and remained there about fifteen months. On leaving, he addressed a letter to Julius, asserting his orthodoxy, and in proof of it reciting the Creed following, which he speaks of as the faith which he had been taught by his forefathers in God out of the Holy Scriptures, and which he himself had been accustomed to preach.

From this account we should have been prepared to look for a Creed framed upon the Eastern model. But the Formulary which he produces lacks the characteristics of the Eastern Creeds: and it is evident, on inspection, that it is the Creed of the Church of Rome; for, with two exceptions, one of which, the omission of Πατέρα in the 1st article, may probably be due to the oversight of the transcriber, it is identical with the Roman Creed, as indicated by Rufinus half a century later. Nor is it to be wondered that, writing to conciliate the good opinion of the Bishop of Rome, he should have expressed his belief in the terms of the Formulary used by the Church of Rome, while in substance the truths which he set forth were none other than those which he had received from his instructors in Christianity. What the language of Marcellus's Creed was originally does not appear. Epiphanius, who wrote in Greek, delivers it in that language [h].

---

[h] This notice is nearly a literal transcript from the author's Harmonia Symbolica, pp. 23, 24.

1. ΠΙΣΤΕΥΩ εἰς Θεὸν παντοκράτορα·
2. Καὶ εἰς Χριστὸν Ἰησοῦν, τὸν Υἱὸν αὐτοῦ τὸν μονογενῆ,
   τὸν Κύριον ἡμῶν,
3. Τὸν γεννηθέντα ἐκ Πνεύματος ἁγίου
   καὶ Μαρίας τῆς Παρθένου,
4. Τὸν ἐπὶ Ποντίου Πιλάτου σταυρωθέντα,
   καὶ ταφέντα,
5. Καὶ τῇ τρίτῃ ἡμέρᾳ ἀναστάντα ἐκ τῶν νεκρῶν,
6. Ἀναβάντα εἰς τοὺς οὐρανούς,
   Καὶ καθήμενον ἐν δεξιᾷ τοῦ Πατρός,
7. Ὅθεν ἔρχεται κρίνειν ζῶντας καὶ νεκρούς·
8. Καὶ εἰς τὸ ἅγιον Πνεῦμα,
9. Ἁγίαν ἐκκλησίαν,
10. Ἄφεσιν ἁμαρτιῶν,
11. Σαρκὸς ἀνάστασιν,
12. Ζωὴν αἰώνιον[1].

VI. AQUILEIA (RUFINUS), *circ.* A.D. 400.

Towards the close of the fourth century or the beginning of the fifth, we have an Exposition of the Creed by Rufinus, a Presbyter of the Church of Aquileia. Rufinus does not give the articles of the Creed on which he comments consecutively; but it is easy to collect them from his text. It is the Creed of his own Church, the Church of Aquileia.

1. CREDO in Deo Patre omnipotente,
   invisibili et impassibili;
2. Et in Christo Jesu, unico Filio ejus,
   Domino nostro,

[1] Epiphanius Hær. 52, al. 72, tom. i. pp. 835, 836. Paris, Ed. 1622.

3. Qui natus est de Spiritu Sancto
   ex Maria Virgine,
4. Crucifixus sub Pontio Pilato,
   et sepultus,
   Descendit ad inferna,
5. Tertia die resurrexit a mortuis,
6. Ascendit ad cœlos,
   Sedet ad dexteram Patris,
7. Inde venturus est judicare vivos et mortuos;
8. Et in Spiritu Sancto,
9. Sanctam Ecclesiam,
10. Remissionem peccatorum,
11. Hujus Carnis resurrectionem [k].

Rufinus's Creed ended with the 11th article [l]. But in his Commentary he explains the Resurrection as being a Resurrection to eternal life: so that the 12th article here, as in some other Creeds, though not expressed, is implied in the 11th [m].

The peculiarity in the 1st article, "invisibili et impassibili," Rufinus tells us, was intended as a protest against the Patripassian heresy, which, confounding the persons of the Father and the Son, held the Incarnation and whatsoever followed upon it to have taken place in the Person of the Father [n].

Rufinus's is the earliest Creed in which the clause, "He descended into Hell," occurs;—the earliest or-

[k] Rufini Commentarius in Symbolum.

[l] Sed et ultimus Sermo iste, qui Resurrectionem carnis pronunciat, summam totius perfectionis succincta brevitate concludit. Rufin. in Symb. § 41.

[m] Ibid. § 45.

[n] Ibid. § 5. On the ablative case instead of the accusative, in Arts 1, 2, 8, see Harmonia Symbolica, p. 27.

thodox Creed, not the earliest Creed absolutely, for it had appeared before in three Arian Formularies[o]. Eventually, but not till after a considerable time, it came to be incorporated universally in the Creeds of the West. In the Eastern Creeds—at least in the orthodox Eastern Creeds—it is never found.

The insertion of the demonstrative pronoun "hujus" in the 11th article, "Hujus carnis resurrectionem," was intended to emphasize the doctrine, which some denied, that this very flesh of which our bodies consist (and people, when reciting the Creed, made the sign of the Cross upon their foreheads when they said the word), this very flesh shall rise again to be made a vessel of honour meet for the Master's use, if it have been kept free from sin, but if otherwise, a vessel of wrath fitted for destruction[p].

VII. ROME, THE 4th AND 5th CENTURIES.

Rufinus, as he proceeds in his Exposition, mentions, from time to time, instances in which the Creed of the Roman Church differed from that of Aquileia. We are thus enabled to construct the Roman Creed, such as it was at the close of the fourth century and the beginning of the fifth; and this (as may be inferred, on the one side, from the Creed of Marcellus above given, and on the other, from quotations and references in the writings of St. Leo, Bishop of Rome from 440 to 461) continued the same from before the middle of the fourth cen-

---

[o] They may be seen in Harmonia Symbolica, p. 135.

[p] Rufin. § 43.

tury till after the middle of the fifth—in all probability during the whole of both centuries. With Marcellus's Creed it agrees almost word for word. Whether it contained Article 12 in express terms, which Marcellus's Creed did, is doubtful. That article was not in the Aquileian Creed, and Rufinus makes no reference to any discrepancy between the Roman and the Aquileian in this particular. It had evidently not as yet become generally established.

1. CREDO in Deum Patrem omnipotentem;
2. Et in Jesum Christum, Filium ejus unicum, Dominum nostrum,
3. Qui natus est de Spiritu Sancto ex Maria Virgine,
4. Crucifixus sub Pontio Pilato, et sepultus,
5. Tertia die resurrexit a mortuis,
6. Ascendit ad cœlos, Sedet ad dexteram Patris,
7. Inde venturus est judicare vivos et mortuos;
8. Et in Spiritum Sanctum,
9. Sanctam Ecclesiam,
10. Remissionem peccatorum,
11. Carnis resurrectionem.

VIII. THE CREED COMPLETE, IN ITS PRESENT FORM.

The preceding Formulary exhibits the Creed as it stood towards the close of the fifth century. In the author's Harmonia Symbolica various other Creeds will be found, all more or less incomplete, of dates ranging from the beginning of the sixth to the middle of the eighth century, when for the first time we meet with a Formulary containing all the clauses of the Creed as we now use it, though even after that date incomplete Formularies still occur. I subjoin it in the complete form in which, with the occasional exceptions referred to, it has continued from the middle of the eighth century to the present day, inclosing in brackets those words or clauses which had no established footing till after the middle or probably the close of the fifth century.

1. Credo in Deum Patrem omnipotentem,
   [Creatorem cœli et terræ;]
2. Et in Jesum Christum, Filium Ejus unicum,
   Dominum nostrum,
3. Qui [conceptus] est de Spiritu Sancto,
   Natus ex Maria Virgine,
4. [Passus] sub Pontio Pilato,
   Crucifixus, [mortuus,] et sepultus,
5. [Descendit ad inferos,]
   Tertia die resurrexit a mortuis,
6. Ascendit ad cœlós,
   Sedet ad dexteram [Dei] Patris [omnipotentis,]
7. Inde venturus est judicare vivos et mortuos;
8. Credo in Spiritum Sanctum,
9. Sanctam Ecclesiam [Catholicam],
   [Sanctorum communionem,]
10. Remissionem peccatorum,
11. Carnis Resurrectionem,
12. [Vitam æternam.]

II. PROBABLE DATES OF ADDITIONS OR ALTERATIONS IN THE SEVERAL ARTICLES.

The following, chiefly from the author's *Harmonia Symbolica*, is a brief historical notice of the several articles, with the probable dates of the additions or alterations which have been made in them.

Art. 1. The clause, "Creatorem cœli et terræ," does not appear in any Western Creed till the seventh century, though Irenæus and Tertullian have what is equivalent. The Eastern Creeds are rarely without it. From them in all probability it found its way into those of the West. It was inserted in order to maintain the truth against those heretics who denied that the Creator of the world and the Father of our Lord Jesus Christ are one and the same.

Art. 2 has remained unaltered from the first, the only variation being that in some instances we have "unigenitum Filium" instead of "unicum."

In Art. 3 the earliest form was, "Natus de Spiritu Sancto et Maria Virgine," or "Natus de Spiritu Sancto ex Maria Virgine." "Conceptus" is of late introduction. It may possibly have been suggested by a sentence of St. Leo's in his Tome [q]; but it does not appear to have been in his Creed. Nor was it generally established even in the latter part of the eighth century [r].

---

[q] "Conceptus quippe est de Spiritu Sancto intra uterum matris Virginis." § 1.

[r] Alcuin, who may be regarded as representing both the Anglo-Saxon and the French Church of the latter half of the eighth century, still uses the earlier form, "Dicitur in Sym-

Art. 4. The earlier Creeds for the most part were content to express simply the Crucifixion and the Burial, implying the Passion in the one, and the Death in the other. The article did not generally reach its present completeness till the seventh century. The name of Pilate occurs almost universally, as marking the time at which our Lord suffered [a].

Art. 5. The clause, "Descendit ad inferna," as I have already observed, occurs for the first time, if we except the Arian Creeds above referred to, in the Creed of Aquileia, at the end of the fourth century. It had then no place in the Roman Creed; but it is found in the Creed commented on by Venantius Fortunatus towards the end of the sixth century, and thenceforward is of frequent occurrence.

The remaining clause, "Tertia die resurrexit a mortuis," has stood as we now have it from the first.

Art. 6. The only change here is that instead of the earlier form, "Sedet ad dexteram Patris," the present, "ad dexteram Dei Patris omnipotentis," has been established since the middle of the seventh century.

Art. 7 has remained unaltered from the first.

So also has Art. 8, "Credo in Spiritum Sanctum,"

bolo Catholicæ Fidei quod Christus de Spiritu Sancto et ex Maria Virgine sit natus." De Trin. iii. 10. And Etherius and Beatus (A.D. 785), representing the Spanish Church, recite the third article, "Qui natus est de Spiritu Sancto et Maria Virgine."

[a] Cautissime qui Symbolum tradiderunt etiam tempus quo hæc sub Pontio Pilato gesta sunt designaverunt, ne ex aliqua purte velut vaga et incerta gestorum traditio vacillaret. Rufin. in Symb. § 18.

except that some of the earliest Creeds leave out the "Credo," contenting themselves with saying simply "et in Spiritum Sanctum," a form naturally agreeing with the state of a text newly formed out of the Baptismal Formulary, when as yet comparatively few clauses intervened between Arts. 2 and 8. "This form," Bishop Bull observes, " expressed the doctrine of the Trinity in a clearer, stronger, and closer manner than some of the more enlarged Creeds afterwards did. For the insertion of additional articles, time after time, carried the words "Son" and "Holy Ghost" so far off from the word "God," that it might look as if that high title, which belonged indifferently to all three, was there applied to the Father only, though the compilers of those larger Creeds really designed the same common application of the name of God as before [t]."

Art. 9. "Sanctam Ecclesiam Catholicam." This clause, but simply as "Sanctam Ecclesiam," has probably had a place in the Creed from the first. "Catholicam" is found in some Creeds of uncertain date, but it does not appear to have become established till the seventh century. In the Eastern Creeds it is of universal occurrence.

Rufinus lays stress on the omission of the preposition "in" before the ninth and following articles, as though it had an important doctrinal significance, and succeeding writers of the Western Church follow in his wake. The Oriental Church usually made no such distinction, though it was not disregarded by some of its divines. Thus, e.g., Gregory Nazianzen

[t] Bull, Judic. Eccles. Cathol. 4, § 3.

rests an argument upon it for the Deity of the Holy Ghost. See Pearson's note at the beginning of his Exposition of Art. 8.

"Sanctorum Communionem" is one of the latest additions. It can hardly be considered as established till the close of the eighth century. It is never found in the Eastern Creeds.

The remaining articles, equally with the clause last mentioned, are all subordinate to and dependent on the "Holy Catholic Church." It is in and through the Church as the Body of Christ, that the saints have communion with each other, obtain Forgiveness of sins, and look for the Resurrection of the flesh unto Eternal Life [n].

Art. 10. "Remissionem peccatorum." This article is of universal occurrence: in the Eastern Creeds often with the specification of Baptism, as the Sacrament of forgiveness.

Art. 11. This article has always had a place in the Creeds, and in the Latin always in the same form, "Resurrectionem carnis," not "corporis." The English Church is peculiar in the use of its word "body," at least in the version with which we are most familiar, the version used in the daily morning and evening services. In the Baptismal Offices and the Order for the Visitation of the Sick, "Resurrectionem car-

---

[n] Unum vestris precibus commendo, ut ab eo qui Catholicus non est animum et auditum vestrum omnimodis avertatis, quo Remissionem peccatorum, et Resurrectionem carnis, et vitam æternam per unam veram et sanctam Ecclesiam Catholicam apprehendere valeatis. S. August. Serm. 215, Opera, tom. v. col. 1385.

nis" is translated literally, "the Resurrection of the flesh."

There was an ambiguity in the Latin language which made "Resurrectionem corporis" a suspicious term in the eyes of the ancient Church, since there were heretics who, while they denied the Resurrection in the strict sense of the word, endeavoured to shelter themselves under the formula, "Resurrectionem corporis," which (the Latin having no article) might mean "the Resurrection of *a* body," not necessarily of *the* body, the very body which had been united to the soul in life. Our language, however, leaves no room for evasion. When we say, "We believe the resurrection of the body," we can mean of no other body than the one which we now have. The Aquileian Church, as we have seen, though it used the word "carnis," which might have seemed sufficiently precise, yet, to leave no possible loophole, prefixed the pronoun "hujus," "hujus carnis Resurrectionem," and the person who recited the Creed made the sign of the Cross upon his forehead while reciting the words.

Art. 12. "Vitam æternam." This article, though appearing in the African Creed of the middle of the third century, is wanting in several Creeds of dates considerably later. It is found in the Creed of Marcellus, presumably the Creed of the Church of Rome, in the middle of the fourth century. But Rufinus's Creed was without it; and he gives no indication that the Roman Creed differed from the Aquileian in this particular. On the whole, it would seem, that for several ages there was no uniform rule respecting it, and that it was not till the middle of the seventh century that it became established as a separate article, distinct from the preceding article, in which, however, when not expressed, it was implied.

III. INTERROGATIVE CREEDS.

It may be well to add a few words on the Interrogative Creeds used at Baptism. These frequently differed more or less from the Declarative Creeds. As a rule, the 3rd and 4th Articles were abridged, and the 5th, 6th, and 7th, omitted. At the same time, as the Declarative Creeds became enlarged by the addition of fresh clauses, the Interrogative Creeds in the Articles which were retained ordinarily kept pace with them.

The following may serve as examples [x]:—

I. CARTHAGE (ST. CYPRIAN), A.D. 246—258.

10. Credis remissionem peccatorum
12. Et vitam æternam
9. Per sanctam Ecclesiam [y] ?
      otherwise
12. Credis in vitam æternam
10. Et remissionem peccatorum
9. Per sanctam Ecclesiam [z] ?

---

[x] Other examples are given in the author's Harmonia Symbolica, pp. 106—116.
  [y] Ad Magnum, Ep. 76.
  [z] Ad Episcopos Numidas, Ep. 70.

II. MILAN (ST. AMBROSE), *circ.* A.D. 380.

Interrogatus es,
1. Credis in Deum Patrem omnipotentem?
    Dixisti, Credo;
    (Et mersisti, hoc est, sepultus es:)
    Iterum interrogatus es,
2. Credis in Dominum nostrum, Jesum Christum,
4. Et in crucem Ejus?
    Dixisti, Credo;
    (Et mersisti; ideo et Christo es consepultus:)
    Tertio interrogatus es,
8. Credis et in Spiritum Sanctum?
    Dixisti, Credo;
    (Tertio mersisti, ut multiplicem lapsum superioris ætatis absolverit trina confessio [a].)

III. ROME (THE GELASIAN SACRAMENTARY), A.D. 495. But in use in France, *circ.* A.D. 750.

1. Credis in Deum Patrem omnipotentem?
    Credo:
2. Credis et in Jesum Christum, Filium Ejus unicum,
    Dominum nostrum,
3. Natum,
4. Et passum?
    Credo:
8. Credis et in Spiritum Sanctum,

---

[a] St. Ambrose, de Sacramentis, l. 2, c. 7, tom. ii. p. 359. Paris, 1686—1690.

9. Sanctam Ecclesiam,
10. Remissionem peccatorum,
11. Carnis resurrectionem?
  Credo [b].

IV. ENGLAND (SALISBURY MANUAL), A.D. 1543.

1. Credis in Deum Patrem omnipotentem,
  Creatorem cœli et terræ?
   Credo:
2. Credis et in Jesum Christum, Filium Ejus unicum,
 Dominum nostrum,
3. Natum,
4. Et passum?
   Credo:
8. Credis et in Spiritum Sanctum,
9. Sanctam Ecclesiam Catholicam,
 Sanctorum communionem,
10. Peccatorum remissionem,
11. Carnis resurrectionem,
12. Vitam æternam post mortem?
   Credo.

V. ENGLAND (BOOK OF COMMON PRAYER),
  BAPTISMAL CREED NOW IN USE [c].

1. Dost thou believe in God the Father Almighty, Maker of heaven and earth?
2. And in Jesus Christ His only-begotten Son, Our Lord?

[b] Muratori, tom. i. p. 570.

[c] Baptismal Services: so also the Order for the Visitation of the Sick.

3. And that He was conceived by the Holy Ghost,
   Born of the Virgin Mary;
4. That He suffered under Pontius Pilate,
   was crucified, dead, and buried;
5. That He went down into Hell,
   and also did rise again the third day;
6. That He ascended into heaven,
   and sitteth at the right hand of God the Father Almighty,
7. And from thence shall come again at the end of the world,
   to judge the quick and the dead?
8. And dost thou believe in the Holy Ghost,
9. The holy Catholic Church,
   The Communion of Saints,
10. The Remission of sins,
11. The Resurrection of the flesh,
12. And everlasting life after death?
    All this I steadfastly believe.

THE APOSTLES'
AND
NICENE CREEDS
HARMONIZED.

LXII.—APOSTLES'.

[The parts without brackets represent, *on the whole*, the Western Creed of the 4th, 5th, and 6th Centuries.]

1. Credo in Deum Patrem omnipotentem,
   [Creatorem coeli et terræ;]

2. Et in Jesum Christum, Filium ejus unicum,
   Dominum nostrum;

3. Qui [conceptus] est de Spiritu Sancto,
   Natus ex Maria Virgine;

4. [Passus] sub Pontio Pilato, crucifixus,
   [mortuus,] et sepultus;
5. [Descendit ad inferna;]
   Tertia die resurrexit a mortuis;
6. Ascendit ad coelos;
   Sedet ad dexteram [Dei] Patris [omnipotentis;]
7. Inde venturus est
   judicare vivos et mortuos.

LXIII.—NICENE. (CONSTANTINOPLE.)
A.D. 381.

[The parts without brackets represent the original Nicæno-Constinopolitan Creed, as accepted and ratified by the Council of Chalcedon.]

1. ΠΙΣΤΕΥΟΜΕΝ εἰς ἕνα Θεὸν Πατέρα παντοκράτορα,
   ποιητὴν οὐρανοῦ καί γῆς,
   ὁρατῶν τε πάντων καὶ ἀοράτων·

2. Καὶ εἰς ἕνα Κύριον, Ἰησοῦν Χριστὸν,
   τὸν υἱὸν τοῦ Θεοῦ τὸν μονογενῆ,
   τὸν ἐκ τοῦ Πατρὸς γεννηθέντα πρὸ πάντων τῶν αἰώνων,
   [Deum de Deo,]
   Φῶς ἐκ Φωτὸς,
   Θεὸν ἀληθινὸν ἐκ Θεοῦ ἀληθινοῦ,
   γεννηθέντα οὐ ποιηθέντα,
   ὁμοούσιον τῷ Πατρί·
   δι' οὗ τὰ πάντα ἐγένετο·

3. Τὸν, δι' ἡμᾶς τοὺς ἀνθρώπους
   καὶ διὰ τὴν ἡμετέραν σωτηρίαν,
   κατελθόντα ἐκ τῶν οὐρανῶν,
   καὶ σαρκωθέντα
   ἐκ Πνεύματος ἁγίου καὶ Μαρίας τῆς Παρθένου,
   καὶ ἐνανθρωπήσαντα·

4. Σταυρωθέντα τε ὑπὲρ ἡμῶν ἐπὶ Ποντίου Πιλάτου,
   καὶ παθόντα, καὶ ταφέντα·

5.   *   *   *
   Καὶ ἀναστάντα τῇ τριτῇ ἡμέρᾳ κατὰ τὰς γραφάς·

6. Καὶ ἀνελθόντα εἰς τοὺς οὐρανούς·
   καὶ καθεζόμενον ἐκ δεξιῶν τοῦ Πατρός·

7. Καὶ πάλιν ἐρχόμενον μετὰ δόξης
   κρίναι ζῶντας καὶ νεκρούς·
   οὗ τῆς βασιλείας οὐκ ἔσται τέλος·

8. Credo in Spiritum Sanctum ;

9. Sanctam Ecclesiam [Catholicam ;
   [Sanctorum communionem ;]
10. Remissionem peccatorum ;
11. Carnis resurrectionem ;
12. [Vitam æternam.]

8. Καὶ εἰς τὸ Πνεῦμα τὸ ἅγιον,
τὸ Κύριον,
καὶ τὸ ζωοποιὸν,
τὸ ἐκ τοῦ Πατρὸς [Filioque] ἐκπορευόμενον,
τὸ σὺν Πατρὶ καὶ Υἱῷ
συμπροσκυνούμενον καὶ συνδοξαζόμενον,
τὸ λαλῆσαν διὰ τῶν προφητῶν·
9. Εἰς μίαν ἁγίαν καθολικὴν καὶ ἀποστολικὴν Ἐκκλησίαν·
* * *
10. Ὁμολογοῦμεν ἓν βάπτισμα εἰς ἄφεσιν ἁμαρτιῶν·
11. Προσδοκῶμεν ἀνάστασιν νεκρῶν,
12. Καὶ ζωὴν τοῦ μέλλοντος αἰῶνος.

CHAPTER III.

CREEDS OF THE EASTERN CHURCH.

HOOKER, E. P., BK. 5, CH. 54, § 10.

THERE are but four things which concur to make complete the whole state of our Lord Jesus Christ: His Deity, His Manhood, the conjunction of both, and the distinction of the one from the other being joined in one. Four principal heresies there are which have in those things withstood the truth: Arians, by bending themselves against the Deity of Christ; Apollinarians, by maiming and misinterpreting what belongeth to His human nature; Nestorians by rending Christ asunder and dividing Him into two Persons; the followers of Eutyches, by confounding in His Person those Natures which they should distinguish.

Against these there have been four most ancient General Councils: the Council of Nice, to define against Arians; against Apollinarians, the Council of Constantinople; the Council of Ephesus, against Nestorians; against Eutychians, the Chalcedon Council. In four words, ἀληθῶς, τελέως, ἀδιαιρέτως, ἀσυγχύτως (the first applied to His being God, the second to His being Man, the third to His being of both one, and the fourth to His still continuing in that one both) we may fully, by way of abridgment, comprise whatsoever antiquity hath at large handled either in declaration of Christian belief, or in refutation of the aforesaid heresies.

CHAPTER III.

CREEDS OF THE EASTERN CHURCH.

DECLARATIVE CREEDS.

I. JERUSALEM.

For the following Creed, from the Baptismal Service of the Church of Jerusalem, we are indebted to St. Cyril, Bishop of that See. St. Cyril's Catechetical Lectures, in the nineteenth of which it is found, were delivered by him, while yet a Presbyter, in the year 347 or 348; but the Creed is so simple in its structure that it may well be believed to be of the highest antiquity, not improbably indeed the original Confession of the mother Church of Christendom.

The Lecture in which it occurs is one of five addressed to a class of newly-baptized persons. St. Cyril reminds his hearers, referring to the Baptismal Service, that they were first conducted into the vestibule of the Baptistery, and were bidden to turn their faces towards the West, that being the region of darkness, and to renounce Satan, saying, with significant gesture, stretching out and spreading asunder their hands,

> Ἀποτάσσομαί σοι, Σατανᾶ,
> καὶ πᾶσι τοῖς ἔργοις σου,
> καὶ πάσῃ τῇ πομπῇ σου,
> καὶ πάσῃ τῇ λατρείᾳ σου.

Then, having thus broken all compact with Satan, they turned round to the East, the region of light, and said:—

1. Πιστεύω εἰς τὸν Πατέρα,
2. καὶ εἰς τὸν Υἱὸν,
3. καὶ εἰς τὸ Ἅγιον Πνεῦμα,
10. καὶ εἰς ἓν βάπτισμα μετανοίας.

They were next conducted into the Baptistery (Catech. xx.), and having been undressed, and anointed with the oil of exorcism, they were placed in the font, and were asked, each severally, εἰ πιστεύει εἰς τὸ ὄνομα τοῦ Πατρὸς, καὶ τοῦ Υἱοῦ, καὶ τοῦ Ἁγίου Πνεύματος; On making confession of this faith, they were plunged three times beneath the water, and immediately afterwards (Catech. xxi. 1) were anointed with ointment, "the antitype of the unction with which Christ was anointed," a sign and token of the Holy Ghost now given them.

It is obvious to trace through this simple Creed the connexion between Creeds of a more complex character and the Baptismal Formula. That Formula is undoubtedly the germ from which the Creed in all its varieties, both Eastern and Western, has been developed, though, as it would seem, the type on which the Eastern Creeds have been formed for the most part is 1 Cor. viii. 6.

> εἷς Θεὸς ὁ Πατὴρ
> ἐξ οὗ τὰ πάντα·
> καὶ εἷς Κύριος, Ἰησοῦς Χριστὸς,
> δι' οὗ τὰ πάντα.

II. III. THE CREED SUBMITTED TO THE COUNCIL OF NICÆA BY EUSEBIUS, BISHOP OF CÆSAREA, AND THE CREED PUT FORTH BY THE COUNCIL—THE NICENE CREED.

A.D. 325.

The Council of Nicæa, A.D. 325, introduces us to a new era in the history of the Creed.

Hitherto the various Churches, which together made up the one Church Catholic, had been content to confess the faith in the Formularies which had been severally handed down to them, though the Eastern Church, by the necessity of the case, had been constrained to be fuller and more precise on more points than one than the Western [a]. But from this time the most jealous and watchful care is apparent. We are conscious at once that we have entered into a country where the assaults of an enemy are continually to be apprehended. If all other history of the fourth century had perished, there would be enough in the Creeds which it produced to shew that the Church, at least the Eastern Church, had had an arduous struggle in maintaining the truth during its progress.

In the year 319, Arius, a presbyter of Alexandria, who had already acquired an evil notoriety by schismatical proceedings [b], but had subsequently been reconciled to the Church, was present one day when Alexander, Bishop of Alexandria, was discoursing before his clergy on the doctrine of the Trinity [c].

---

[a] Rufin. in Symb. § 3. [b] Sozom. i. 15.

[c] Φιλοτιμότερον περὶ τῆς ἁγίας Τριάδος, ἐν Τριάδι Μονάδα εἶναι φιλοσοφῶν, ἐθεολόγει. Socr. i. 5.

Arius questioned the soundness of his teaching. He said that it was Sabellian, and he proceeded to expound his own view. Pressing the analogy between divine and human sonship, as though it held at every point, and overlooking the teaching of Scripture direct and indirect, he urged that if the Father begat the Son, then the Son had a beginning of existence, ἀρχὴν ὑπάρξεως ἔχει ὁ γεννηθείς : consequently there was when He was not, ἦν ὅτε οὐκ ἦν· He had His being from non-entity, ἐξ οὐκ ὄντων ἔχει τὴν ὑπόστασιν· in one word, He was a creature [d].

The term "Son," as applied to our blessed Lord, was in truth the pivot on which the controversy was made to turn. The Arians inferred from it that, as in human sonship a son's existence is posterior to his father's, so in the Divine likewise. The Son of God therefore must have had a beginning of existence, however remote its date. "There was when He was not." They did not say there was "a time;" "they dropped the word 'time,'" St. Athanasius says, "to deceive the simple [e]."

The Catholics inferred from the word "Son" that as in the human sphere sonship implies identity of nature, so in the Divine likewise. The Son of God, therefore, must be of the same nature as His Father, God, as His Father is God.

[d] For Arius's own account of his teaching see his Letter to Eusebius of Nicomedia, Theodoret i. 5, also his Thalia, as quoted by St. Athanasius, De Synodis ii. 15. With it may be compared Bishop Alexander's account in his Letter to the bishops of the Catholic Church, Socrates i. 6, and in his Letter to his namesake, Alexander, Bp. of Constantinople, Theodoret i. 4.   [e] Contra Arianos iv. 13.

The question, however, is not to be determined by such reasoning, but by the teaching of Holy Scripture. The Arians did not disregard the Scriptural argument, but, as Alexander says of them, collecting together passages which speak of our Lord in terms proper to the humiliation to which for our sake He submitted, they took no notice, except to explain them away, of others which speak of His Divine majesty and glory[f].

Alexander for a time bore with his Presbyter. But at length, when the evil leaven began to spread, he summoned a meeting of his clergy, in which Arius was permitted to state and defend his belief, while the Catholics maintained that the Son is of one substance and one eternity with the Father, ὁμοούσιος καὶ συναίδιος.

Alexander still forbore to act with decision, till at length matters proceeded so far that they roused both him and the Church generally. A synod, consisting of nearly a hundred bishops of Libya and Egypt, was assembled, and Arius was excommunicated with his followers. This was about the year 320. The heresy, however, continued to spread. It extended itself through the whole of Egypt, Libya, and the Upper Thebais; then it ravaged the other provinces, till the strife of words enlisted not only the clergy but the laity also, and the matter became so notorious,

[f] Alexander's Epistle in Theodoret I. c. iv. For a detailed account of the Arian argument see Newman's Arians of the Fourth Century, Chap. ii. § 5. Of this work and of the notes in the Oxford Translation of St. Athanasius much use has been made in the following pages.

that even in the heathen theatres Christianity was made a laughing-stock [g].

It was not long before notice of this state of things reached the ears of Constantine, who was then at Nicomedia [h]. He wrote a letter to Alexander and Arius jointly, exhorting them to compose their differences, and to forbear to enter into the discussion of questions so abstruse and inscrutable [i].

This letter, however, failed of its object, and Constantine was advised to summon a general Council, σύνοδος οἰκουμενική, which might once for all settle the question in dispute [k].

Accordingly there met at Nicæa in Bithynia, in the summer of 325, upwards of three hundred bishops, besides a number of the inferior clergy, brought together from all parts of Christendom, but chiefly from the Eastern provinces. Eusebius gives the names and sees of several of them; the principal being Hosius, Bp. of Cordova, who acted as President, Alexander, Bp. of Alexandria, attended by his Deacon, Athanasius, Eustathius, Patriarch of Antioch, Macarius of Jerusalem, Marcellus of Ancyra, to whom, as above

[g] Socr. Eccl. Hist. i. 6.

[h] It was at Nicomedia, in the palace built by Diocletian, that Constantine was baptized on his death-bed, A.D. 337.

[i] Soc. i. 7. Euseb. de Vita Constant. II. 68 sqq. See Newman's remarks on Constantine and on this letter, Arians III. 1, and Bp. Kaye, Council of Nicæa, p. 25. The bearer of the letter was Hosius, Bishop of Cordova.

[k] This was not the only object for which the Council was assembled. Another was the settling of the Paschal Controversy. Eusebius indeed, in his Life of Constantine, gives the latter so great prominence, that his reader might easily suppose it to have been the only object.

noticed, we are indebted for the earliest complete form of the Western Creed which has come down to us. Though a strenuous maintainer of the orthodox doctrine at the Council, he afterwards became tainted with heresy [1]. The number of Arian bishops is variously stated at thirteen, seventeen, and twenty-two, the most conspicuous of them being the well-known prelates of Cæsarea and Nicomedia, both of whom bore the name of Eusebius [m].

The result of their deliberations, so far as the subject before us is concerned, was the promulgation of the Creed, which, in the strictest sense, is entitled to be called the "Nicene Creed." It had the assent of 318 bishops, from which circumstance it is frequently designated the Creed of the 318 [n]. Socrates gives it at length [o]. Sozomen, though he relates the history of the Council and its proceedings, withholds the Creed of set purpose. It had been his intention, he says, to insert it; but his friends had dissuaded him, fearing the exposure of the Christian doctrine to the uninitiated [p].

[1] St. Athanasius, who is disposed to defend him, classes him with others whom the Arians persecuted for being orthodox. Apol. contr. Arian. ii. 20. Histor. Arian. i. 7. See note on the former passage in the Oxf. Transl., p. 52.

[m] Newman, Arians of the Fourth Century, Ch. iii. § 1.

[n] The Fathers delighted to recognize in this number a coincidence with the number of Abraham's trained servants with whom he smote the confederate kings, and rescued Lot. Moreover in the Greek letters $\tau\iota\eta$, which express that number, they saw in τ the form of the Cross, in $\iota\eta$ the two first letters of our Saviour's name. "Crux in trecentis, Jesu nomen in decem et octo." St. Ambrose, de Fide, i. 18, 122.

[o] Socr. i. 8.   [p] Soz. i. 20.

The first draught of the Creed was a Formulary presented to the Council by Eusebius, Bp. of Cæsarea, in the early part of its deliberations. Such at least Eusebius himself states to have been the case, and a comparison between it and the Creed eventually agreed upon confirms his statement.

"We have thought good," he says, in a letter to the people of his diocese [q], "to send you first the Formulary proposed by ourselves, then the Creed, which they published, containing certain terms added to ours (ἣν ταῖς ἡμετέραις φωναῖς προσθήκας ἐπιβαλόντες ἐκδεδώκασι)." "The Formulary submitted by us," he continues, after first reciting it, "was received without opposition (οὐδενὶ παρῆν ἀντιλογίας τρόπος). It was suggested, however, that the word ὁμοούσιον should be inserted, and the suggestion pressed on the Council by Constantine was agreed to."

Tillemont (Tom. 6. 655) and Valesius (in his notes on Theodoret I. vii. viii.) regard this claim of Eusebius in behalf of the Creed which he had presented, as an empty boast, referring for proof to Theodoret's account and Eustathius's in Theodoret, of a Creed presented by the Arians, which the Fathers of the Council rejected with indignation and tore in pieces forthwith. Neander, however, suggests, with great probability, that this was a Creed presented by the other Eusebius, Eusebius of Nicomedia [r].

Eusebius's Creed was not indeed a private Formulary of his own composing, but, as he tells us, the Creed of the Church of Cæsarea, over which he presided. It was "the faith which he had received from

---

[q] Socr. i. 8.   [r] Neander, Ecc. Hist. iv. p. 22 n.

the bishops who preceded him, first when he was being instructed as a Catechumen, and afterwards when he was baptized. Such also he had learnt from the Holy Scriptures, such he had believed, such he had taught, first as presbyter, afterwards as bishop." He then recites it, and proceeds to justify himself to the people of his diocese for having subscribed the Formulary promulgated by the Council.

The Creed agreed upon by the Council is sometimes said to have been the production of Hosius. So it was stated by his Arian opponents, when seeking to prejudice the Emperor Constantius against him [a]. The only sense in which this can be true is that probably it was chiefly through Hosius's influence that the Creed submitted by Eusebius was altered to the form eventually accepted.

II. THE CREED SUBMITTED TO THE COUNCIL OF NICÆA BY EUSEBIUS, BISHOP OF CÆSAREA.— A.D. 325. Socr. H. E. i. 8.

1. ΠΙΣΤΕΥΟΜΕΝ εἰς ἕνα Θεὸν πατέρα παντοκράτορα,
 τὸν τῶν ἁπάντων, ὁρατῶν τε καὶ ἀοράτων, ποιητήν·

2. Καὶ εἰς ἕνα Κύριον, Ἰησοῦν Χριστόν,
 Τὸν τοῦ Θεοῦ Λόγον,
 Θεὸν ἐκ Θεοῦ,
 Φῶς ἐκ Φωτὸς,
 Ζωὴν ἐκ Ζωῆς,
 Υἱὸν μονογενῆ,
 πρωτότοκον πάσης κτίσεως,
 πρὸ πάντων τῶν αἰώνων ἐκ τοῦ Θεοῦ Πατρὸς γεγενν-
 ημένον·

[a] Athanas. Histor. Arianorum, c. vi.

δι' οὗ καὶ ἐγένετο τὰ πάντα·
3. Τὸν διὰ τὴν ἡμετέραν σωτηρίαν
σαρκωθέντα,
καὶ ἐν ἀνθρώποις πολιτευσάμενον,
4. Καὶ παθόντα,
5. Καὶ ἀναστάντα τῇ τρίτῃ ἡμέρᾳ,
6. Καὶ ἀνελθόντα πρὸς τὸν Πατέρα,
7. Καὶ ἥξοντα πάλιν ἐν δόξῃ
κρῖναι ζῶντας καὶ νεκρούς·
8. Πιστεύομεν καὶ εἰς ἓν Πνεῦμα Ἅγιον·

III. THE CREED OF THE COUNCIL OF NICÆA.
A.D. 325. SOCRATES, H. E. i. 8.

1. ΠΙΣΤΕΥΟΜΕΝ εἰς ἕνα Θεὸν Πατέρα παντοκράτορα,
πάντων ὁρατῶν τε καὶ ἀοράτων ποιητήν·
2. Καὶ εἰς ἕνα Κύριον, Ἰησοῦν Χριστὸν,
τὸν Υἱὸν τοῦ Θεοῦ,
γεννηθέντα ἐκ τοῦ Πατρὸς μονογενῆ,
τουτέστιν ἐκ τῆς οὐσίας τοῦ Πατρὸς,
Θεὸν ἐκ Θεοῦ,
Φῶς ἐκ Φωτὸς,
Θεὸν ἀληθινὸν ἐκ Θεοῦ ἀληθινοῦ,
γεννηθέντα, οὐ ποιηθέντα,
ὁμοούσιον τῷ Πατρί·
δι' οὗ τὰ πάντα ἐγένετο, τά τε ἐν τῷ οὐρανῷ καὶ τὰ ἐν τῇ γῇ·
3. Τὸν δι' ἡμᾶς τοὺς ἀνθρώπους καὶ διὰ τὴν ἡμετέραν
σωτηρίαν
κατελθόντα,
καὶ σαρκωθέντα,
καὶ ἐνανθρωπήσαντα,

4. Παθόντα,
5. Καὶ ἀναστάντα τῇ τρίτῃ ἡμέρᾳ,
6. Ἀνελθόντα εἰς τοὺς οὐρανοὺς,
7. Καὶ πάλιν ἐρχόμενον
Κρῖναι ζῶντας καὶ νεκρούς·
8. Καὶ εἰς τὸ Πνεῦμα τὸ Ἅγιον·

ΤΟΥΣ δὲ λέγοντας, Ἦν ποτὲ ὅτε οὐκ ἦν, καὶ πρὶν γεννηθῆναι οὐκ ἦν, καὶ ὅτι ἐξ οὐκ ὄντων ἐγένετο, ἢ ἐξ ἑτέρας ὑποστάσεως ἢ οὐσίας φάσκοντας εἶναι, ἢ κτιστὸν, ἢ τρεπτὸν, ἢ ἀλλοιωτὸν τὸν Υἱὸν τοῦ Θεοῦ, τούτους ἀναθεματίζει ἡ καθολικὴ καὶ ἀποστολικὴ ἐκκλησία.

It will have been observed that both of these Creeds end with the 8th Article, καὶ εἰς τὸ Πνεῦμα τὸ Ἅγιον, and some have thought from this circumstance that the Oriental Creeds generally lacked the remaining Articles[t]. But there is no warrant for this supposition.

In the ancient Jerusalem Creed (above, p. 50) we have the 10th Article, in St. Irenæus's Creed (above, p. 20), which, though Western in locality is Eastern in form, the 11th. In the Creed of the Apostolical Constitutions (below, p. 74), we have the 9th, 10th, 11th, and 12th. In the Creed of Alexandria (below, p. 67), so far as it may be collected from the Letter of its Bishop, Alexander, and this a contemporary document, we have the 9th and 11th. So early as five years after the Council, Articles 9, 11, and 12 occur in the Creed which Arius and Euzoius presented to Constantine (below, p. 68). The Creed of Jeru-

---

[t] Bull, Judic. Eccles. Cath. vi. 8.

salem, some twenty years later, A.D. 347 or 348 (below, p. 75), contains all the four.

The remaining Articles then were not wanting in the Church's Creed antecedently to the Nicene Council; but the subjects to which those Articles relate not being in dispute at the time, the Fathers of the Council did not think it necessary to re-state them. As St. Jerome says, "They affirmed what was denied, they were silent as to what no one questioned ⁿ."

If we compare the Creed put forth by the Council with the Creed submitted by Eusebius, the only difference of importance will be found in the 2nd Article. In itself Eusebius's Creed was unexceptionable ˣ. It

---

ⁿ Confessi sunt quod negabatur, tacuerunt de quo nemo quærebat. Epist. ad Pam. et Ocean.

ˣ "Though the words ἐκ τῆς οὐσίας and ὁμοούσιος were omitted, every term of honour and dignity short of these was bestowed upon the Son of God, who was designated as the Λόγος of God, 'Light of Light,' 'Life of Life,' 'the only-begotten Son,' 'the First-born of the whole Creation,' 'made of the Father before all worlds,' and the Instrument of creating them. The three Persons were confessed to be in real existence, i.e. in opposition to Sabellianism, and to be ἀληθινῶς Father, Son, and Holy Ghost. The Catholics saw very clearly that concessions of this kind, on the part of the Arians, did but conceal the real question in dispute. Orthodox as were the terms employed by them, naturally and satisfactorily as they would have answered the purpose of a test, had the existing questions never been agitated, and consistent as they were with certain producible statements of the Ante-Nicene writers, they were irrelevant, at a time when evasions had been found for them all and triumphantly proclaimed." Newman, Arians, ch. iii. § 1. See Bp. Kaye's Remarks, Council of Nicæa, p. 48.

contained nothing to which the most orthodox could
have objected. But it failed to strike the heresy
which was making havoc of the Church. The Arians,
putting their own sense upon its phrases, could have
signed it without hesitation. If it spoke of the Son
as "the Word of God," "the First-born of every
creature," these were Scriptural expressions, and they
had their own way of explaining them. If it declared
that "He was begotten of God the Father," they
could say, "We too are of God;" and as to the
"before all worlds," they held that He was begotten
in order to create the world. They had no difficulty
on these points[y].

[y] "When the bishops were desirous," says Athanasius, "of
ridding the Church of the impious expressions invented by
Arius, τὸ ἐξ οὐκ ὄντων, τὸ κτίσμα λέγειν τὸν Υἱόν, τὸ ἦν ποτὲ ὅτε
οὐκ ἦν, ὅτι τρεπτῆς ἐστι φύσεως, and perpetuating those which
we receive on the authority of Scripture, that the Son is ἐκ
Θεοῦ φύσει μονογενής, as the Apostle John says, and as Paul
"the Radiance of His glory," and "the express image of His
Person," the Eusebians said one to another, "Let us agree to
this, for we too are ἐκ Θεοῦ, there being one God, of whom are
all things.... The bishops, however, discerning their cunning
and the artifice adopted by their impiety, in order to express
more clearly the ἐκ τοῦ Θεοῦ, wrote down ἐκ τῆς οὐσίας τοῦ Θεοῦ,
of the substance of God, creatures being spoken of as ἐκ τοῦ
Θεοῦ, as not existing of themselves without cause, but having
a beginning of production, but the Son being peculiarly ἐκ
τῆς τοῦ Πατρὸς οὐσίας.... Last of all, they expressed themselves more clearly and concisely in the phrase ὁμοούσιον εἶναι
τῷ Πατρὶ τὸν Υἱόν, for all that was before said has this meaning. As to their complaint about non-scriptural phrases, they
themselves refute it. It was they who began with their
impious expressions, τὸ ἐξ οὐκ ὄντων, and τὸ ἦν ποτὲ ὅτε οὐκ ἦν,
which are not in Scripture, and now they make it a charge,

It was necessary, therefore, to find a formula which should express the proper Deity of the Son of God with a precision which would admit of no evasion. For this, St. Ambrose tells us, they were indebted to the other Eusebius, Eusebius of Nicomedia, one of the chief supporters of Arius. "If," said he, "we affirm that Christ, the Word, the Son of God, is also uncreated, we necessarily confess Him to be "of one substance, ὁμοούσιος, with the Father." The Council took the hint, and forthwith inserted the phrase in the Creed, that they might, so to speak, slay the enemies of the truth with their own sword[s].

It was this phrase then, ὁμοούσιος, "of one substance," and the phrase ἐκ τῆς οὐσίας, used a little before to explain μονογενής, that formed the essential difference between the Creed formulated by the Council and the Creed presented by Eusebius, and, it should seem, all previous Creeds. Thenceforward ἐκ τῆς οὐσίας and ὁμοούσιος became the symbols of orthodoxy, as regards the nature of the Second Person of the Sacred Trinity. The Arians, however they might explain away and put a non-natural sense upon other expressions, could never, unless they would be openly false, adopt these.

Eusebius, though in his Life of Constantine he hastens over that part of the history of the Council which relates to the Arian controversy, goes at some length, in his Letter to the People of Cæsarea, into

that they are detected by means of non-scriptural terms, which have been reverently adopted." St. Athanasius, ad. Afros, 5, 6, as translated in Newman's Arians, ch. ii. § 5.

[s] St. Ambros. De Fide iii. cap. 44.

the discussion of the word ὁμοούσιος and the propriety of its insertion in the Creed*.

It appears that not a few had scruples with regard to it. Nor was this to be wondered at. It had been used by heretics in a heretical sense. Moreover, it had been deliberately repudiated in a synod held at Antioch some sixty years previously. But when the Arians denied the truth, which the word, rightly understood, symbolised, the Nicene Fathers recalled it. It was urged against it that it was not to be found in Holy Scripture, to which Athanasius replied that, on the one hand, neither were the Arian For-

* Eusebius's Letter should be read attentively for his comments on the additions made by the Council. They were far from welcome to him, and his first impulse was to withhold his acquiescence. But he discovered a mode of explaining them such as to satisfy his conscience, and, as he hoped, to justify him in the eyes of his people. See the notes upon it in the Oxford Translation of Athanasius, pp. 59 sqq. Eusebius had so far espoused the cause of Arius as to receive him when excommunicated by Alexander, shortly before the Council, and had not hesitated to declare his concurrence with him to the full extent of his heresy. He had even denied that our Lord is ἀληθινὸς Θεός. Newman, Arians, p. 137. Arius, in his letter to Eusebius of Nicomedia, claims him, together with other Eastern bishops, as symbolising with himself in his belief. Theodoret i. 5. Yet "in Eusebius's own writings," Mr. Newman says, "there is very little that fixes on him any charge beyond that of an attachment to the Platonic phraseology. Had he not connected himself with the Arian party, it would have been unjust to suspect him of heresy. The grave accusation under which he lies is not that of Arianising, but of corrupting the simplicity of the Gospel with an Ecclectic spirit. While he held out the ambiguous language of the schools as a refuge, his conduct gave countenance to the secular maxim,

mulæ, "of things that were not," &c., and on the other, that though the word was not in Scripture, yet the sense of it was, and that the Council was constrained to use it, there being no other term which could hold the subtle and slippery adversaries with whom they had to deal [b].

With regard to the sense in which it was used by the Council, this may be gathered sufficiently from the Creed itself. The word, as its etymology indicates, and as it was employed by approved Greek writers, signifies "of the same substance or essence," οὐσία being the substance or essence of which a thing consists, that which it is. In this sense then, only avoiding the idea of *materiality* [c], as though οὐσία meant substance in our popular sense, and strenuously maintaining but one οὐσία, the Council employed the term to signify that such as the Father is, such is the Son likewise, the Father God, the Son God, both in the same august sense, and yet not two Gods, but one God. For after declaring the Son to be μονογενής, "the only-begotten of the Father," they continue,

that difference of Creeds is a matter of inferior moment, and that provided we express our belief in the very words of Scripture, we may speculate as philosophers, and live as the world." Arians, p. 150. In his note on Eusebius's Letter, however, Mr. Newman takes a much more unfavourable view of his tenets. Oxford Translation of Athanasius, pp. 62, &c. Bp. Kaye, Council of Nicæa, p. 44, speaks more leniently of him.

[b] See Bull, Def. Fid. Nic. 2, 1, 9, sqq.

[c] It is perhaps to be lamented that "substance" rather than "essence" has become the ordinary English rendering of οὐσία.

"that is, of the substance or essence of the Father," and this they further explain by "God of God," "Light of Light," "Very God of Very God," "Begotten not made," and then, as though to sum up all that had gone before in one comprehensive phrase, they add "of one substance with the Father [d]."

So again, in the anathema appended to the Creed they anathematise those who say "that the Son is of a different substance or essence from the Father," "that once He did not exist," "that He was created," "that He is alterable, subject to change," all of which are negations direct or indirect of what they intend by affirming that the Son is "of one substance with the Father."

It is a question whether the words οὐσία and ὑπόστασις in the anathema are to be understood as interchangeable, both signifying "substance" or "essence," or whether they are to be taken in different senses. Bp. Bull maintains the latter view against Petavius [e]. Mr. Newman examines, and successfully, it would seem, controverts Bp. Bull's arguments [f].

There was at first an indeterminateness in the use

---

[d] Recte ὁμοούσιον Patri Filium dicemus, quia verbo eo et Personarum distinctio et Naturæ unitas significatur. St. Ambros. de Fide, III. 126. 'Ομοούσιος implied a difference as well as unity, Ταυτοούσιος implied, with the Sabellians, an identity or a confusion. Newman, Oxford Translation of St. Athanasius, p. 208 n.

[e] Def. Fid. Nic. II. ix. 11.

[f] Oxf. Translation of St. Athanasius's Treatises against the Arians, pp. 63 sqq. At pp. 272 sqq. he discusses the meaning of the Arian Formula, πρὶν γεννηθῆναι οὐκ ἦν, on which also see Bp. Bull, Def. Fid. Nic. III. ix. 2.

F

of ὑπόστασις. Sometimes it was used as equivalent to οὐσία, at others as equivalent to what is meant by "Persona." But the Latins, rendering it etymologically "substantia," were scandalized when they found the Greeks speaking of τρεῖς ὑποστάσεις, as though they meant three "substances;" and there was for some time danger of a schism. But at length they came to an understanding, and thenceforward ὑπόστασις was restricted to the sense of "Person"[f].

IV. THE CREED OF ALEXANDRIA, AS COLLECTED FROM THE LETTER OF ITS BISHOP, ALEXANDER, TO ALEXANDER, BISHOP OF CONSTANTINOPLE. A.D. 323. THEODORET, i. 4.

Before leaving the Nicene Council and its Creed, it may be well to add the following fragments, collected from a letter addressed by Alexander, Bishop of Alexandria, to his namesake, the Bishop of Constantinople, written on the first outbreak of Arius's heresy.

Alexander indeed does not say, in so many words, that he is quoting from any definite Formulary; he simply says that he is stating the faith as it is accepted by the Church; but it is evident that he is to a considerable extent using the precise words of the Creed with which he was familiar, the Creed of his own branch of the Church.

Ἡμεῖς οὕτως πιστεύομεν, ὡς τῇ ἀποστολικῇ ἐκκλησίᾳ δοκεῖ.

1. εἰς μόνον ἀγένητον Πατέρα . . .
2. καὶ εἰς ἕνα Κύριον Ἰησοῦν Χριστόν,

[f] See Newman's Arians of the Fourth Century, ch. v. § 2, and Suicer in v.

τὸν υἱὸν τοῦ Θεοῦ τὸν μονογενῆ . . .

3. Σῶμα φορεσάντα ἀληθῶς καὶ οὐ δοκήσει ἐκ Θεοτόκου Μαρίας[h],

ἐπὶ συντελείᾳ τῶν αἰώνων, εἰς ἀθέτησιν ἁμαρτίας,

4. Σταυρωθέντα καὶ ἀποθανόντα,

5. Ἀναστάντα ἐκ νεκρῶν,

6. Ἀναληφθέντα ἐν οὐρανοῖς,

Καθήμενον ἐν δεξιᾷ τῆς μεγαλωσύνης.

8. Ὁμολογοῦμεν ἓν Πνεῦμα Ἅγιον,

9. Μίαν καὶ μονὴν καθολικὴν τὴν ἀποστολικὴν ἐκκλησίαν.

11. Ἀνάστασιν ἐκ νεκρῶν.

V. THE CREED EXHIBITED BY ARIUS AND EUZOIUS TO CONSTANTINE, A.D. 330. Socr. i. 26.

Arius, at the close of the Nicene Council, had been banished to Illyria. But it was represented to Constantine by a certain Presbyter whom his sister Constantia had recommended to him on her deathbed, and who had gained an ascendancy over him, that Arius had been hardly dealt with. On this Constantine wrote to Arius, inviting him to Constantinople, and on his arrival, accompanied by Euzoius[i], a deacon, whom the Bishop of Alexandria had deposed at the same time with Arius[k], commanded him to give him a declaration of his faith in

---

[h] Note the use of the epithet Θεοτόκος a century before the rise of Nestorianism.

[i] Euzoius afterwards was made Bishop of Antioch by the Arian party. Constantius was baptized by him. Jerome adv. Lucif. referred to by Bishop Kaye, Council of Nicæa, p. 17, n. 4. [k] Theodor. i. 4.

writing. This he did, and Constantine was so well satisfied that he sent him to Alexandria, and directed Athanasius, now become its bishop, to receive him again into the Church[1].

Some have supposed the formulary in question to be the normal creed of Alexandria, of which Arius was a presbyter [m]; but a comparison with the foregoing fragments gathered from Alexander's letter does not confirm the supposition. Arius's Creed is as follows:—

1. ΠΙΣΤΕΥΟΜΕΝ εἰς ἕνα Θεὸν Πατέρα παντοκράτορα.

2. Καὶ εἰς Κύριον Ἰησοῦν Χριστὸν,
τὸν Υἱὸν αὐτοῦ,
τὸν ἐξ αὐτοῦ πρὸ πάντων τῶν αἰώνων γεγεννημένον,
Θεὸν,
Λόγον
Δι' οὗ τὰ πάντα ἐγένετο, τά τε ἐν τοῖς οὐρανοῖς καὶ τὰ ἐπὶ τῆς γῆς,

3. τὸν κατελθόντα,
καὶ σαρκωθέντα,

4. καὶ παθόντα,

5. καὶ ἀναστάντα,

6. καὶ ἀνελθόντα εἰς τοὺς οὐρανοὺς

7. καὶ πάλιν ἐρχόμενον κρῖναι ζῶντας καὶ νεκρούς·

8. καὶ εἰς τὸ Ἅγιον Πνεῦμα.

---

[1] This Athanasius refused to do, notwithstanding a threatening letter with which Constantine followed up his injunction. Socr. Hist. Eccl. l. i. cc. 25, 26, 27.

[m] So Ussher, Suicer, Bingham, and others.

11. καὶ εἰς σαρκὸς ἀνάστασιν,
12. καὶ εἰς ζωὴν τοῦ μέλλοντος αἰῶνος,
καὶ εἰς βασιλείαν οὐρανῶν·
9. καὶ εἰς μίαν καθολικὴν ἐκκλησίαν τοῦ Θεοῦ
τὴν ἀπὸ περάτων ἑὼς περάτων.

ΤΑΥΤΗΝ δὲ τὴν πίστιν παρειλήφαμεν ἐκ τῶν ἁγίων εὐαγγελίων, λέγοντος τοῦ Κυρίου τοῖς ἑαυτοῦ μαθηταῖς· Πορευθέντες μαθητεύσατε πάντα τὰ ἔθνη, βαπτίζοντες αὐτοὺς εἰς ὄνομα τοῦ Πατρὸς καὶ τοῦ Υἱοῦ καὶ τοῦ Ἁγίου Πνεύματος.

"This faith we have received from the Holy Gospels, wherein the Lord says to His disciples, 'Go and make disciples of all nations, baptizing them into the Name of the Father, and of the Son, and of the Holy Ghost.' That we thus believe these statements, and receive in sincerity the Father, the Son, and the Holy Ghost, as the whole Catholic Church and the Scriptures, which we believe in all points, teach, God is our judge, both now and in the judgment to come."

This Creed might well impose upon Constantine. It was in fact so ambiguously worded, and the precise point in controversy so studiously kept out of view, that without committing its author to statements at variance with his opinions, it served the purpose of concealing sentiments which he felt it inconvenient to avow. Arius had no hesitation in acknowledging our Blessed Lord to be God, to have been begotten before the world, to have made all things, provided only that these statements were accepted in his own sense.

This consideration will enable us to understand how it came to pass that Athanasius and those who sided with him clung so persistently to the phrases, ἐκ τῆς οὐσίας τοῦ Πατρὸς and ὁμοούσιος τῷ Πατρί, when, in so doing, they seemed to be disturbing the peace of the Church for the sake of a word, nay, as the case was put, of a letter. The fact is, these formulæ were the only tests which the Arians were unable to evade. They were the safeguards by which the truth, that the Son is very God, God in the truest and highest sense, was protected. It is easy to speak slightingly of the struggle which was maintained through the greater part of the fourth century, as though it were a mere strife of words, but such language betrays great ignorance of human nature. Words and the things which they represent are intimately connected. And it has happened again and again, both in secular history and in ecclesiastical, that an important truth has been furtively withdrawn from men's grasp, when apparently all that has been taken away has been a word or a syllable.

VI. THE CREED OF THE APOSTOLICAL CONSTITUTIONS (4th century), CONSTIT. APOST. VII. § 41.

Nothing certain is known as to the date and authorship of the Apostolical Constitutions. The work, as Bishop Pearson suggests[o], is evidently

---

[o] Fuerunt, ex sententia nostra, antiquitus hi libri, quasi ab Apostolis scripti aut dictati, Διδαχὴ Ἀποστόλων, Διατάξεις Ἀποστόλων, Διδασκαλία Κλήμεντος, Διδασκαλία Ἰγνατίου, Διδασ-

a patchwork, made up of documents belonging to various periods, with additions, interpolations, and retrenchments, intended to bring it into conformity with the beliefs of the several compilers and the customs of their times, the basis of it, at all events of the first 32 sections of the 7th Book, being without doubt the Διδαχὴ 'Αποστόλων recently brought to light P.

Epiphanius (A.D. 373) quotes it in several instances: but it is not clear that he was acquainted with more than the first six books; nor is the text which he cites identical in every instance with that which we now read; in one instance it is opposed to it. (Epiph. Hær. lxx. §§ 10, 11, compared with Apost. Const. v. § 17.) He speaks of the work with respect. But it had already fallen under the suspicion of having been tampered with, and it is not improbable that after his time it was rendered still further liable to the charge. It was on this ground condemned by the Trullan Council (A.D. 692), Αἷς τισι πάλαι ὑπὸ τῶν ἑτεροδόξων ἐπὶ λύμῃ τῆς 'Εκκλησίας νόθα τινὰ καὶ ξένα τῆς εὐσεβείας παρενέτεθησαν·

The Creed familiarly known as the Creed of the Apostolical Constitutions is found in what now forms the 7th Book of that work. It contains one clause, τὸν πρὸ αἰώνων εὐδοκίᾳ τοῦ Πατρὸς γεννηθέντα, evidently

καλία δὶ Ἱππολύτου, Διδαχὴ Πολυκάρπου. Ex his omnibus et aliis fortasse adhuc incognitis conflatæ sunt Διαταγαὶ sive Καθολικὴ Διδασκαλία. Vindic. Ignat. i. 4.

P See Bryennius, Διδαχὴ τῶν δώδεκα 'Αποστόλων, § ϛ', and Professor Swainson's Greek Liturgies, pp. xlvi. &c., in each of which the correspondence between the two documents is exhibited.

of an Arian character [q], which points to a date subsequent to the rise of that heresy, and another, οὗ τῆς βασιλείας οὐκ ἔσται τέλυς, which points to a date subsequent to the rise of the heresy of Marcellus of Ancyra [r], who denied the eternity of Christ's Kingdom. On these grounds, though the work has often been referred to the close of the third century, by some even to an earlier date [s], I venture to place its Creed between that of Arius and that of Cyril of Jerusalem.

The Creed belongs to the Baptismal Service, and is preceded by directions for the instruction of the Catechumens who are being prepared for that Sacrament [t]."

The Catechumen is to be instructed in the knowledge of the unoriginate Father, of the Only-begotten Son, and of the Holy Ghost. He is to be taught why the world was made, and why man, the citizen of the world, ὁ κοσμοπολίτης, was created. He is to have explained to him how God punished the wicked spirits with fire and water, and how He glorified His saints in each succeeding generation, such as Seth, Enoch, Noah, Abraham, &c. . . . and when the time

[q] Arius in his account of his belief, says of the Son, ὅτι θελήματι καὶ βουλῇ ὑπέστη, πρὸ χρόνων καὶ αἰώνων, πλήρης Θεός. Letter to Eusebius of Nicomedia, Theodor. i. 5. See Newman's Arians, Ch. ii. § 5.

[r] Cyril Hieros. xv. § 27. Also Ch. iv. § 15, and Rufin. in Sym. § 39.

[s] Whiston in his "Primitive Christianity Revived," referred it to the age of the Apostles, and went so far as to class it with the Canonical Scriptures.

[t] Apostol. Constit. vii. 39, 40.

of baptism is at hand he is to be taught the necessity of renouncing the world and entering into covenant with Christ. For as the husbandman first cleanses his field from weeds and then sows his wheat, so God's ministers must first extract all ungodliness, and then administer baptism. For thus the Lord commanded, First "make disciples of all nations," then "baptize them in the Name of the Father, and of the Son, and of the Holy Ghost."

Let him then who is to be baptized say,

> Ἀποτάσσομαι τῷ Σατανᾷ,
> καὶ τοῖς ἔργοις αὐτοῦ,
> καὶ ταῖς πομπαῖς αὐτοῦ,
> καὶ τοῖς ἀγγέλοις αὐτοῦ,
> καὶ ταῖς ἐφευρέσεσιν αὐτοῦ,
> καὶ πᾶσι τοῖς ὑφ᾽ αὐτοῦ.

Having thus renounced Satan, let him enter into covenant with Christ, saying,

> Συντάσσομαι τῷ Χριστῷ, καὶ βαπτίζομαι
> 1. Εἰς ἕνα ἀγέννητον, μόνον, ἀληθινὸν Θεὸν, παντοκράτορα,
>   τὸν Πατέρα τοῦ Χριστοῦ,
>   κτίστην καὶ δημιουργὸν τῶν ἁπάντων,
>   ἐξ οὗ τὰ πάντα·
> 2. Καὶ εἰς τὸν Κύριον Ἰησοῦν τὸν Χριστὸν,
>   τὸν μονογενῆ αὐτοῦ Υἱὸν,
>   τὸν πρωτότοκον πάσης κτίσεως,
>   τὸν πρὸ αἰώνων εὐδοκίᾳ τοῦ Πατρὸς γεννηθέντα,
>   [οὐ κτισθέντα]
>   δι᾽ οὗ τὰ πάντα ἐγένετο, τὰ ἐν οὐρανοῖς καὶ ἐπὶ γῆς,
>   ὁρατά τε καὶ ἀόρατα·

3. Τὸν ἐπ' ἐσχάτων ἡμερῶν κατελθόντα ἐξ οὐρανῶν,
καὶ σάρκα ἀναλαβόντα,
καὶ ἐκ τῆς ἁγίας παρθένου Μαρίας γεννηθέντα,
καὶ πολιτευσάμενον ὁσίως κατὰ τοὺς νόμους
τοῦ Θεοῦ καὶ Πατρὸς αὐτοῦ,

4. Καὶ σταυρωθέντα ἐπὶ Ποντίου Πιλάτου,
καὶ ἀποθανόντα ὑπὲρ ἡμῶν,

5. Καὶ ἀναστάντα ἐκ νεκρῶν μετὰ τὸ παθεῖν
τῇ τρίτῃ ἡμέρᾳ,

6. Καὶ ἀνελθόντα εἰς τοὺς οὐρανούς,
καὶ καθεσθέντα ἐν δεξιᾷ τοῦ Πατρός,

7. Καὶ πάλιν ἐρχόμενον, ἐπὶ συντελείᾳ τοῦ αἰῶνος, μετὰ δόξης,
κρῖναι ζῶντας καὶ νεκρούς,
οὗ τῆς βασιλείας οὐκ ἔσται τέλος·

8. Βαπτίζομαι καὶ εἰς τὸ Πνεῦμα τὸ Ἅγιον,
τουτέστι τὸν Παράκλητον,
τὸ ἐνεργῆσαν ἐν πᾶσιν τοῖς ἀπ' αἰῶνος ἁγίοις,
ὕστερον δὲ ἀποσταλὲν καὶ τοῖς ἀποστόλοις παρὰ
τοῦ Πατρός, κατὰ τὴν ἐπαγγελίαν τοῦ Σωτῆρος
ἡμῶν, Κυρίου Ἰησοῦ Χριστοῦ, καὶ μετὰ τοὺς
ἀποστόλους δὲ πᾶσι τοῖς πιστεύουσιν·

9. Ἐν τῇ ἁγίᾳ καθολικῇ ἐκκλησίᾳ·

11. Εἰς σαρκὸς ἀνάστασιν.

10. Καὶ εἰς ἄφεσιν ἁμαρτιῶν·

12. Καὶ εἰς βασιλείαν οὐρανῶν,
καὶ εἰς ζωὴν τοῦ μέλλοντος αἰῶνος.

VII. THE CREED OF JERUSALEM [u], A.D. 347 or 348.

The exposition of faith put forth at Nicæa was followed by a number of creeds drawn up by the Arian party, or by one or another of the subdivisions into which it soon split. Amid many variations, these are all cast in the same mould as the orthodox Formulary, only in the 2nd Article they are framed so as either to express the heretical tenets of their authors, or else to conceal them under vague generalities [x].

Leaving these, I proceed to the Creed of Jerusalem, expounded by St. Cyril in his Lectures to the Catechumens whom he was preparing for baptism. St. Cyril does not give the creed continuously. But it is easy to collect the several portions of it from his exposition, and put them together.

1. ΠΙΣΤΕΥΟΜΕΝ εἰς ἕνα Θεὸν, Πατέρα παντοκράτορα,
 ποιητὴν οὐρανοῦ καὶ γῆς, ὁρατῶν τε πάντων καὶ ἀοράτων·

2. Καὶ εἰς ἕνα Κύριον, Ἰησοῦν Χριστὸν,
 τὸν Υἱὸν τοῦ Θεοῦ τὸν μονογενῆ,
 τὸν ἐκ τοῦ Πατρὸς γεννηθέντα Θεὸν ἀληθινὸν
 πρὸ πάντων αἰώνων,
 δι' οὗ τὰ πάντα ἐγένετο·

3. Ἐν σαρκὶ παραγενόμενον,
 καὶ ἐνανθρωπήσαντα
 ἐκ Παρθένου καὶ Πνεύματος Ἁγίου·

---

[u] Collected from S. Cyril's Catechetical Lectures.

[x] They are to be seen in St. Athanasius de Synodis, c. 2, and Hilary de Synodis.

4. Σταυρωθέντα,
   καὶ ταφέντα,
5. Ἀναστάντα τῇ τρίτῃ ἡμέρᾳ,
6. Καὶ ἀνελθόντα εἰς τοὺς οὐρανούς,
   καὶ καθίσαντα ἐκ δεξιῶν τοῦ Πατρὸς
7. Καὶ ἐρχόμενον ἐν δόξῃ,
   κρῖναι ζῶντας καὶ νεκρούς,
   οὗ τῆς βασιλείας οὐκ ἔσται τέλος·
8. Καὶ εἰς ἓν Ἅγιον Πνεῦμα,
   τὸν Παράκλητον,
   τὸ λαλῆσαν ἐν τοῖς προφήταις·
10. Καὶ εἰς ἓν βάπτισμα μετανοίας εἰς ἄφεσιν ἁμαρτιῶν.
9. Καὶ εἰς μίαν ἁγίαν καθολικὴν Ἐκκλησίαν·
11. Καὶ εἰς σαρκὸς ἀνάστασιν·
12. Καὶ εἰς ζωὴν αἰώνιον.

It will be observed that St. Cyril's Creed does not contain the crucial formulæ, ἐκ τῆς οὐσίας and ὁμοούσιος, but there is nothing in his Exposition inconsistent with them. The Creed which he was expounding was doubtless the Creed of his Church, such as it was before the Nicene Council. Such it probably continued for some time afterwards, till, as in the case of other Churches, it was superseded by the Nicene, and eventually by the Constantinopolitan [y].

VIII. IX. EPIPHANIUS'S CREEDS, A.D. 373.

The two following Creeds are preserved by Epiphanius in his Anchorate, "The Anchored One,"

[y] See Touttée's Dissertation at the end of St. Cyril of Jerusalem's 5th Catechesis, p. 82.

a work written at the request of certain Presbyters and other members of the Church of Pamphylia, who had sought from him a statement of Christian Doctrine, for the confutation of heresies then prevalent, and for the establishment in the faith of some who were in danger of drifting from their moorings.

The former of these Creeds, which is identical, save in two particulars, with the Constantinopolitan, he attributes, after the Apostles, to the Fathers of the Nicene Council—such at least seems to be the meaning of his words—Αὕτη μὲν ἡ πίστις παρεδόθη ἀπὸ τῶν ἁγίων ἀποστόλων, καὶ ἐν ἐκκλησίᾳ τῇ ἁγίᾳ πόλει, ἀπὸ πάντων ὁμοῦ τῶν ἁγίων ἐπισκόπων, ὑπὲρ τριακοσίων δέκα τὸν ἀριθμόν.

The second Creed is an expansion of the former, as that was of the original Nicene Formulary, enlarging especially the 3rd and 8th Articles, with an eye, in the one case to the Apollinarian heresy, in the other to the Macedonian. It is noteworthy as exhibiting the Greek Formula for expressing the relationship of the Holy Spirit to the Father and the Son—"ἐκ τοῦ Πατρὸς ἐκπορευόμενος, καὶ ἐκ τοῦ Υἱοῦ λαμβανόμενος," which the Western Creed expresses by "a Patri Filioque procedens."

"Cease not," Epiphanius says, in concluding his treatise, "Cease not, faithful and orthodox men, to guard and keep this holy faith which the Church received from the holy apostles of the Lord; and not only teach the Catechumens who are preparing for baptism to believe the same, but teach them to express it in the precise words of our common mother —yours and ours:

VIII.

1. ΠΙΣΤΕΥΟΜΕΝ εἰς ἕνα Θεὸν Πατέρα παντοκράτορα,
ποιητὴν οὐρανοῦ τε καὶ γῆς, ὁρατῶν τε πάντων καὶ
ἀοράτων·
2. Καὶ εἰς ἕνα Κύριον, Ἰησοῦν Χριστὸν,
τὸν Υἱὸν τοῦ Θεοῦ τὸν μονογενῆ,
τὸν ἐκ τοῦ Πατρὸς γεννηθέντα πρὸ πάντων τῶν αἰώνων,
τουτέστιν ἐκ τῆς οὐσίας τοῦ Πατρὸς,
Φῶς ἐκ Φωτὸς,
Θεὸν ἀληθινὸν ἐκ Θεοῦ ἀληθινοῦ,
γεννηθέντα, οὐ ποιηθέντα,
ὁμοούσιον τῷ Πατρί·
δι' οὗ τὰ πάντα ἐγένετο, τά τε ἐν τοῖς οὐρανοῖς καὶ τὰ
ἐν τῇ γῇ·
3. Τὸν δι' ἡμᾶς τοὺς ἀνθρώπους καὶ διὰ τὴν
ἡμετέραν σωτηρίαν
κατελθόντα ἐκ τῶν οὐρανῶν,
καὶ σαρκωθέντα
ἐκ Πνεύματος Ἁγίου καὶ Μαρίας τῆς Παρθένου,
καὶ ἐνανθρωπήσαντα·
4. σταυρωθέντα τε ὑπὲρ ἡμῶν ἐπὶ Ποντίου Πιλάτου,
καὶ παθόντα,
καὶ ταφέντα,
5. Καὶ ἀναστάντα τῇ τρίτῃ ἡμέρᾳ,
κατὰ τὰς γραφὰς,
6. Καὶ ἀνελθόντα εἰς τοὺς οὐρανοὺς,
καὶ καθεζόμενον ἐκ δεξιῶν τοῦ Πατρὸς,
7. Καὶ πάλιν ἐρχόμενον μετὰ δόξης
κρῖναι ζῶντας καὶ νεκροὺς,
οὗ τῆς βασιλείας οὐκ ἔσται τέλος·

8. Καὶ εἰς τὸ Πνεῦμα τὸ Ἅγιον,
    Κύριον,
    καὶ ζωοποιόν,
    τὸ ἐκ τοῦ Πατρὸς ἐκπορευόμενον,
    τὸ σὺν Πατρὶ καὶ Υἱῷ συμπροσκυνούμενον καὶ συνδοξαζόμενον,
    τὸ λαλῆσαν διὰ τῶν προφητῶν·
9. Εἰς μίαν ἁγίαν καθολικὴν καὶ ἀποστολικὴν Ἐκκλησίαν·
10. Ὁμολογοῦμεν ἓν βάπτισμα εἰς ἄφεσιν ἁμαρτιῶν·
11. Προσδοκῶμεν ἀνάστασιν νεκρῶν,
12. Καὶ ζωὴν τοῦ μέλλοντος αἰῶνος· ἀμήν.

ΤΟΥΣ δὲ λέγοντας, Ἦν ποτὲ ὅτε οὐκ ἦν, καὶ πρὶν γεννηθῆναι οὐκ ἦν, ἢ ὅτι ἐξ οὐκ ὄντων ἐγένετο, ἢ ἐξ ἑτέρας ὑποστάσεως ἢ οὐσίας φάσκοντας εἶναι ῥευστὸν ἢ ἀλλοιωτὸν τὸν τοῦ Θεοῦ Υἱόν, τουτοὺς ἀναθεματίζει ἡ καθολικὴ καὶ ἀποστολικὴ Ἐκκλησία.

Epiphanius proceeds: "But forasmuch as divers heresies have sprung up in our age[a]," therefore you and we and all the orthodox bishops, in a word the whole Catholic Church, having an eye to the said heresies, enjoin those who are candidates for baptism to profess their faith in the words which follow, agreeably with the aforesaid formula [b],—

IX.

1. ΠΙΣΤΕΥΟΜΕΝ εἰς ἕνα Θεὸν Πατέρα παντοκράτορα,
    πάντων, ἀοράτων τε καὶ ὁρατῶν, ποιητήν·

[a] The 10th year of Valentinian and Valens, and the 6th of Gratian, i.e. A.D. 873.   [b] Epiphan. Ancor. §§ cxix.—cxxi.

2. Καὶ εἰς ἕνα Κύριον, Ἰησοῦν Χριστὸν,
   τὸν Υἱὸν τοῦ Θεοῦ,
   γεννηθέντα ἐκ Θεοῦ Πατρὸς μονογενῆ,
   τουτέστιν ἐκ τῆς οὐσίας τοῦ Πατρὸς,
   Θεὸν ἐκ Θεοῦ,
   Φῶς ἐκ Φωτὸς,
   Θεὸν ἀληθινὸν ἐκ Θεοῦ ἀληθινοῦ,
   γεννηθέντα οὐ ποιηθέντα,
   ὁμοούσιον τῷ Πατρί·
   δι' οὗ τὰ πάντα ἐγένετο, τα τε ἐν τοῖς οὐρανοῖς
   καὶ τὰ ἐν τῇ γῇ, ὁρατά τε καὶ ἀόρατα·
3. Τὸν δι' ἡμᾶς τοὺς ἀνθρώπους καὶ διὰ τὴν ἡμετέραν
        σωτηρίαν
   κατελθόντα,
   καὶ σαρκωθέντα,
   τουτέστι γενηθέντα τελείως
   ἐκ τῆς ἁγίας Μαρίας τῆς ἀειπαρθένου
   διὰ Πνεύματος Ἁγίου,
   ἐνανθρωπήσαντα,
   τουτέστι τέλειον ἄνθρωπον λαβόντα,
   ψυχὴν καὶ σῶμα καὶ νοῦν καὶ πάντα, εἴ τι ἔστιν ἄνθρω-
        πος, χωρὶς ἁμαρτίας,
   οὐκ ἀπὸ σπέρματος ἀνδρὸς
   οὐδὲ ἐν ἀνθρώπῳ,
   ἀλλ' εἰς ἑαυτὸν σάρκα ἀναπλάσαντα εἰς μίαν ἁγίαν
        ἑνότητα,
   οὐ καθάπερ ἐν προφήταις ἐνέπνευσέ τε καὶ ἐλάλησε
        καὶ ἐνήργησεν,
   ἀλλὰ τελείως ἐνανθρωπήσαντα·
   ὁ γὰρ Λόγος σὰρξ ἐγένετο,
   οὐ τροπὴν ὑποστὰς,
   οὐδὲ μεταβαλὼν τὴν ἑαυτοῦ Θεότητα εἰς ἀνθρωπότητα,

εἰς μίαν συνενώσαντα ἑαυτοῦ ἁγίαν τελειότητά τε καὶ Θεότητα,

εἷς γάρ ἐστιν Κύριος Ἰησοῦς Χριστὸς καὶ οὐ δύο,

ὁ αὐτὸς Θεὸς, ὁ αὐτὸς Κύριος, ὁ αὐτὸς βασιλεύς·

4. Παθόντα δὲ τὸν αὐτὸν ἐν σάρκι,

5. Καὶ ἀναστάντα,

καὶ ἀνελθόντα εἰς τοὺς οὐρανοὺς ἐν αὐτῷ τῷ σώματι,

ἐνδόξως καθίσαντα ἐν δεξιᾷ τοῦ Πατρός·

7. Ἐρχόμενον ἐν αὐτῷ τῷ σώματι ἐν δόξῃ

κρῖναι ζῶντας καὶ νεκροὺς,

οὗ τῆς βασιλείας οὐκ ἔσται τέλος·

8. Καὶ εἰς τὸ Ἅγιον Πνεῦμα πιστεύομεν,

τὸ λαλῆσαν ἐν νόμῳ,

καὶ κηρύξαν ἐν τοῖς προφήταις,

καὶ καταβὰν ἐπὶ τὸν Ἰορδάνην,

λαλοῦν ἐν ἀποστόλοις,

οἰκοῦν ἐν ἁγίοις·

οὕτως δὲ πιστεύομεν ἐν Αὐτῷ,

ὅτι ἐστὶ Πνεῦμα ἅγιον,

Πνεῦμα Θεοῦ,

Πνεῦμα τέλειον,

Πνεῦμα παράκλητον,

ἄκτιστον,

ἐκ τοῦ Πατρὸς ἐκπορευόμενον,

καὶ ἐκ τοῦ Υἱοῦ λαμβανόμενον καὶ πιστευόμενον·

9. Πιστεύομεν εἰς μίαν καθολικὴν καὶ ἀποστολικὴν ἐκκλησίαν·

10. Καὶ εἰς ἓν βάπτισμα μετανοίας·

11. Καὶ εἰς ἀνάστασιν νεκρῶν,

καὶ κρίσιν δικαίαν ψυχῶν καὶ σωμάτων·

12. Καὶ εἰς βασιλείαν οὐρανῶν,

καὶ εἰς ζωὴν αἰώνιον.

ΤΟΥΣ δὲ λέγοντας, Ὅτι ἦν ποτὲ ὅτε οὐκ ἦν ὁ Υἱὸς ἢ τὸ Πνεῦμα τὸ Ἅγιον, ἢ ὅτι ἐξ οὐκ ὄντων ἐγένετο, ἢ ἐξ ἑτέρας ὑποστάσεως ἢ οὐσίας φάσκοντας εἶναι τρεπτὸν, ἢ ἀλλοιωτὸν, τὸν Υἱὸν τοῦ Θεοῦ ἢ τὸ Ἅγιον Πνεῦμα, τούτους ἀναθεματίζει ἡ καθολικὴ καὶ ἀποστολικὴ ἐκκλησία, ἡ μήτηρ ὑμῶν τε καὶ ἡμῶν. Καὶ πάλιν ἀναθεματίζομεν τοὺς μὴ ὁμολογοῦντας ἀνάστασιν νεκρῶν, καὶ πάσας τὰς αἱρέσεις τὰς μὴ ἐκ ταύτης τῆς ὀρθῆς πίστεως οὔσας.

IX. THE CONSTANTINOPOLITAN CREED, A.D. 381.

This Creed, notwithstanding its name, certainly was not framed by the Council of Constantinople[c]. It is, as was observed above, identical, with only two exceptions, with the former of the two Creeds contained in Epiphanius's Ancorate, written in 373, eight years before the Council. Whether indeed it even had the sanction of the Council has been questioned. The Acts of the Council are lost, and the Creed, though appended to the Canons in some records, is wanting in others. No mention appears to have been made of it at Ephesus, it is not referred to by Socrates, Sozomen, or Theodoret. It comes before us for the first time at the Council of Chalcedon, when, in the second session, it is read after the Creed of Nicæa, and is described as the Faith publicly set forth by the 150 holy fathers, i.e. by the Council of Constantinople[d]. The Chalcedon Fathers

---

[c] It is said to have been framed by Gregory of Nyssa. Niceph. Eccl. Hist. 1. xii. 8.

[d] Labbe, IV. col. 842.

accepted and ratified it, and inserted it in their Definition of Faith.

It has then the explicit sanction of a General Council, and for all practical purposes, so far as its authority is concerned, it is of no consequence whether that sanction was given for the first time at Chalcedon, or whether the Chalcedon sanction was but an iteration of the sanction already given to it at Constantinople.

It has been suggested that the Creed is based not upon the Nicene but upon the Jerusalem Formulary. The Chalcedon Fathers certainly regarded it simply as an enlargement of the Nicene on those points on which the recent heresies of Apollinaris and Nestorius had made greater precision necessary. "Οὐκ ὥς τι λεῖπον," they say, "not as supplying any thing lacking in the Nicene Formulary, but as recording in express words our belief concerning the Holy Spirit, in opposition to those who are endeavouring to set aside His Sovereignty (δεσποτείαν)," i.e. who represent Him as a ministering spirit, instead of acknowledging Him to be Κύριος, Lord in the same sense in which the Father is Lord, and the Son is Lord.

The truth would seem to be, that though some of the additions were borrowed from the Jerusalem Creed, the basis on which the Constantinopolitan Creed was framed was the Nicene. And accordingly, from very early times, it has been usual to speak of it as the Nicene Creed, when there has been no special reason for distinguishing it from the original Nicene Formulary.

Apollinaris or Apollinarius, Bishop of the Syrian Laodicea, had been, before he fell into heresy, one of the brightest ornaments of the Church of his day, eminent in piety, and distinguished as a champion of the orthodox faith. Epiphanius speaks of his fall as an event which astonished and shocked every one, and indeed seemed past belief till room was no longer left for doubting it[e].

His heresy related to the human nature of our Lord, and in effect denied its verity. He held that, whereas man consists of body, soul (the animal soul, ψυχή, *anima*), and spirit (the rational soul, νοῦς, *animus*), our Lord possessed the two former, but not the last, the Divine Word, the Λόγος, supplying its place. He held also, and this was the error specially contemplated and provided against in the Creed, that the flesh of Christ existed before His appearance on earth, and was not received from His mother[f]. Accordingly, whereas in the original Nicene Creed the third article had stood, Τὸν δι᾽ ἡμᾶς τοὺς ἀνθρώπους καὶ

---

[e] Hæres, lxxvii. p. 996.

[f] Apollinaris seems to have wavered in his opinion, one while holding the truth, at another receding from it. "At one time he acknowledged that the Son received His flesh from the Holy Virgin, at another he affirmed that He brought it with Him from Heaven, at another, that He was born flesh, having received nothing from us." Theodor. v. 8. De carne Christi, sic a recta fide dissensisse perhibentur Apollinaristæ, ut dicerent carnem illam et Verbum unius ejusdemque substantiæ contentiosissime asseverantes, Verbum carnem factum, hoc est, Verbi aliquid in carnem fuisse conversam atque mutatam, non autem carnem de Mariæ carne fuisse susceptam. S. August. de Hæress. f. 55.

διὰ τὴν ἡμετέραν σωτηρίαν, κατελθόντα, καὶ σαρκωθέντα, καὶ ἐνανθρωπήσαντα, the Constantinopolitan Fathers added ἐκ τῶν οὐρανῶν after κατελθόντα, and between σαρκωθέντα and ἐνανθρωπήσαντα, inserted ἐκ Πνεύματος Ἁγίου καὶ Μαρίας τῆς Παρθένου [g].

The clause in the 7th article, οὗ τῆς βασιλείας οὐκ ἔσται τέλος, had already appeared in the Creeds of Jerusalem and the Apostolical Constitutions. It was directed, as has already been said, against the heresy of Marcellus of Ancyra, who taught that at the end of the world the Son will cease to reign, having been Himself resolved again into the Father, and having ceased to have a distinct personal subsistence [h].

But the most important addition to the original Nicene Creed was the addition in the 8th Article, made with an eye to the Macedonian heresy.

Macedonius had been Bishop of Constantinople, but had been deposed, A.D. 360, by a synod held in that city and sent into exile. He formed the sect of the Πνευματόμαχοι, so called from their denial of the Deity of the Holy Ghost. Arius himself, in denying the proper Deity of the Son, by consequence denied that of the Holy Spirit also, speaking of Him as the creature of a creature, κτίσμα κτίσματος. But his chief assault being

[g] So Diogenes, Bishop of Cyzicum, at the Council of Chalcedon. "The Fathers at Nicæa said simply σαρκωθέντα; but the holy Fathers, their successors, i.e. the Fathers at Constantinople, explained the meaning of the word, by adding ἐκ Πνεύματος Ἁγίου καὶ Μαρίας τῆς Παρθένου." Labbe, Vol. 4, col. 136. Evagr. II. 18.

[h] Pearson on the Creed, Art. 6, notes.

upon the Deity of the Son, the Nicene Fathers had left the Article touching the Holy Ghost as they found it. Now, however, that the Deity of the Holy Ghost was more pointedly impugned, it became necessary to declare the truth more explicitly. This was one object proposed to itself by the Council of Constantinople, and the fact of its being so lends confirmation to the common belief that the so-called Constantinopolitan Creed had the sanction of that Council. The Nicene Fathers had been content to say simply, Καὶ εἰς τὸ Πνεῦμα τὸ Ἅγιον. There was now added

τὸ Κύριον,
καὶ τὸ ζωοποιὸν,
τὸ ἐκ τοῦ Πατρὸς ἐκπορευόμενον.
τὸ σὺν Πατρὶ καὶ Υἱῷ συμπροσκυνούμενον καὶ συνδοξαζόμενον
τὸ λαλῆσαν διὰ τῶν προφητῶν.

Here then we have an explicit affirmation of the Deity of the Holy Ghost. He is called "the Lord," Κύριος in the highest sense, as that name is used for Jehovah in the Old Testament, and this, in opposition to the heresy which regarded Him as but a Minister of the Father, such in fact as are the holy angels[1].

---

[1] 2 Cor. iii. 18. Macedonius taught that the Son was in all respects, even κατ' οὐσίαν, ὅμοιον τῷ Πατρί, but that the Holy Ghost was ἄμοιρον τῶν αὐτῶν πρεσβείων, διάκονον καὶ ὑπηρέτην καλῶν αὐτόν, such in fact as are the holy angels. Sozom. iv. 27. See S. August. de Hæress. Vol. 8, col. 54.

He is described further as the "Giver of Life," τὸ ζωοποιόν [k].

And in accordance with these high titles, it is appropriately added that "with the Father and the Son He is jointly worshipped and jointly glorified."

The last clause, "who spake by the Prophets," already had a place in the Creed of Jerusalem. It was from thence probably that it was transferred to the Constantinopolitan. It was directed against those heretics who held that the Old Testament was the work of an evil and malignant Being [l]. It might at first sight seem misplaced, as forming so tame a close to the array of lofty ascriptions which precede it. Apparently, however, in the original draft the Article had stood simply καὶ εἰς τὸ Πνεῦμα τὸ ἅγιον, τὸ λαλῆσαν διὰ τῶν προφητῶν. The insertion afterwards of the now intervening clauses carried the clause τὸ λαλῆσαν διὰ τῶν προφητῶν to the distance at which it now stands from the words to which it was originally joined [m].

[k] John vi. 63 : 2 Cor. iii. 6: Rom. viii. 2.

[l] Manes, e.g., and the Gnostics. See Cyril. Hieros. Cat. vi. § 27 and iv. § 33. The Benedictine Editor, on the latter place, gives a number of references.

[m] So Bishop Bull, Judic. Eccles. Cath. p. 147, Sæpe olim miratus sum, quod Patres Constantinopolitani, in Symbolo suo, post verba illa de Spiritu Sancto, τὸ κύριον, &c., addiderint, τὸ λαλῆσαν διὰ τῶν προφητῶν. Scilicet, post tam magnifica Spiritui Sancto tributa, frigida mihi videbatur adjectio illa 'Qui locutus est, &c.' Verum postquam intellexi vetus Symbolum Orientale habuisse τὸ παράκλητον, τὸ λαλῆσαν διὰ τῶν προφητῶν, ita mecum statui, sanctam synodum, loco, τοῦ τὸν παράκλητον, substituisse magnifica ista, quo veram Spiritus

One other point remains to be noticed. The Creed, as it is now used throughout the Western Church, affirms that the Holy Ghost proceeds "from the Son" as well as from the Father. The Creed in its original form made no mention of the procession "from the Son." Nor has the addition ever had the sanction of an œcumenical council, or been acquiesced in by the Eastern Church.

The precise time when the interpolation was first made is involved in obscurity. Its earliest occurrence is usually ascribed to a creed recited together with the Nicene Symbol and the larger portion of the Coalcedon Definition, at the 3rd Council of Toledo (A.D. 589). But some doubt rests on the genuineness of the text in this particular. The Cologne Edition of the Councils (1530), and the Paris (1535), omit it, and D'Aguirre, though he admits the words, notes in his margin, "Desunt exc."

Dr. Pusey, as appears from his Preface to his son's Translation of St. Cyril of Alexandria and from his own work, "On the Clause 'and the Son,'" seems not to have been aware of the questionableness of the reading in the Toledo text. Believing it genuine, he thinks it probable that Recared and his bishops accepted and used the interpolated Creed in good faith, not doubting that it was in accordance with the text of the original.

But it is more probable that the addition, if made in that Council, was made advisedly and of purpose,

Sancti divinitatem, adversus Macedonium, clarius exprimerent, deinde subjecisse τὸ λαλῆσαν διὰ τῶν Προφητῶν, quod hæc in veteri symbolo sequerentur.

in order to intensify the assertion of the orthodox doctrine. The Fathers had the original text before their eyes in the Chalcedon Definition (see below, p. 111), from which they make a large extract, beginning with the part which follows the Nicene and Constantinopolitan Creeds. The Nicene, however, they give, not as it stands in the Definition, but in accordance with the original text; the Constantinopolitan they give also, not as it stands in the Definition, but, besides other variations both from it and from the original, with the Filioque interpolated. Could they have inserted the interpolation in ignorance [n]?

Dr. Pusey himself furnishes an additional reason for believing that Recared and his bishops were not ignorant of the original text. He tells us (p. 49) that among other enactments they enjoin that "the Constantinopolitan Creed be sung before the Lord's Prayer in all the Churches of Gallæcia, according to the form of the Eastern Church." At pp. 184, 185, he quotes a certain John, Abbot of Biclaro, a person in high esteem with Recared, by whom, shortly after the Council, he was made Bishop of Girone, as recording in his Chronicle the institution of this custom in

---

[n] The following is the text of the Constantinopolitan Creed, recited at the Council, as given by D'Aguirre. I mark the variations. It will be observed that "Deum de Deo" which was not in the original is inserted in the 2nd Article, and that, as in the Creed in our Communion Office, "sanctam" is omitted in the 9th Article. D'Aguirre in his margin, however, notices that "sanctam" is read in the printed copies. "Credimus in unum Deum, Patrem omnipotentem, Factorem cæli et terræ, visibilium omnium et invisibilium *conditorem;* Et in unum

the Eastern Churches, some twenty years previously, by the younger Justin. Now this same John of Biclaro had only recently returned from Constantinople, where he had spent seventeen years. Is it improbable that it was from him that the Spanish Council learnt the custom of the Eastern Churches? Could they, with him among them, though he was not actually of the Council, have been ignorant of the text of the Creed as sung at Constantinople, i.e. in its uninterpolated form?

Be the case as it may, however, there can hardly be a doubt that the insertion of the Filioque, whenever made, was made in Spain in the first instance. From Spain it passed to France, and from France to England[o]. The Roman Church long hesitated before accepting it. Leo III., when urged to sanction it by

---

Dominum Jesum Christum. Filium Dei unigenitum, ex Patre natum ante omnia sæcula, *DEUM EX DEO*, Lumen ex lumine, Deum verum ex Deo vero, natum non factum, homousion Patri, *hoc est, ejusdem substantiæ cum Patre*, per Quem omnia facta sunt, *quæ in cælo et quæ in terra*, Qui propter nos ... et propter nostram salutem, descendit ... et incarnatus est de Spiritu Sancto ex Maria Virgine, homo factus. ... Passus est sub ... Pilato, sepultus; Tertia die resurrexit; ... Ascendit in Cœlos, Sedet ad dextram Patris, Iterum venturus ingloria, judicare vivos et mortuos, Cujus regni non erit finis.

Credimus et in Spiritum Sanctum, Dominum et vivificantem, ex Patre *ET FILIO* procedentem, cum Patre et Filio adorandum et glorificandum, Qui locutus est per Prophetas.

In unam ... Catholicam Apostolicam Ecclesiam; Confitemur unum Baptisma in remissionem peccatorum; Expectamus resurrectionem mortuorum, et vitam futuri sæculi.

[o] Dr. Swete (History of the Procession, p. 19) conjectures that "the Western view of the Procession was received by the

the legates sent by Charlemagne from the Synod of
Aix, A.D. 809, refused to do so, though acknowledging
the truth of the doctrine; and to add weight to his
refusal, and for the safeguard of the genuine text, he
caused the Creed to be engraved on two silver tablets,
on one in Greek, on the other in Latin, which he set
up in a conspicuous place in the Church of St. Paul p.

"Not long afterwards, however," to quote Bp.
Pearson's words, "the following Popes, more in love
with their own authority than desirous of the peace
and unity of the Church, neglected the tables of Leo,
and admitted the addition. This was first done in the
time, and by the power of Pope Nicolas the first, who,
by the activity of Photius, was condemned for it q."

English nation at its first conversion as an integral part of the
faith, and that the Anglo-Saxons, like the Spanish Visigoths,
had never known any other expression of the mystery." This
may be true as regards the *doctrine*, of the knowledge and
acceptance of which as early as A.D. 680 we have distinct
proof in the profession of faith agreed upon at the great Synod
of Heathfield, Bede, E. H. iv. 18, but it is more than doubtful
whether Augustine could have brought with him (A.D. 597) the
Creed in its interpolated form. Dr. Swete has an interesting
note illustrating the tenacity with which the English Church
has always clung to the Filioque, p. 191.

The Filioque occurs in the Anglo-Saxon version of the Constantinopolitan Creed, appended to the Cambridge MS. of
Ælfric's Homilies (circ., 1030), " Se gaeth of tham Fæder and
of tham Suna." I am not aware of any earlier Anglo-Saxon
version still extant, with or without the clause.

p There are some discrepancies in the accounts as to details,
" but whenever the inscription was made, and wherever it was
placed, all agree that Leo adopted this method for preserving
the Creed inviolate." Dr. Swete, p. 225.

q Pearson, On the Creed, Article 8, notes. Vossius, who goes

The insertion was one of the chief causes, or rather occasions, of the unhappy schism between the Greek and Latin Churches, "the Greeks either denying or suspecting the truth of the doctrine, and being very zealous for the authority of the ancient Councils, complained of the Latins, that they had taken upon them to make an addition to a Creed sanctioned by a General Council, and that, in spite of a Canon of another Council, which forbade all additions."

The complaint was not without reason. For though the doctrine is founded on Scripture, and was indeed acknowledged, though under another formula[r], by the earlier Greek Fathers, yet it was not justifiable in one branch of the Church to make an addition to a Creed which had the sanction of the Church Universal, in direct opposition to the reclamation of another and not less important branch[s].

into the matter at some length, ascribes the introduction of the clause on the part of the Roman Church to Sergius, who held the See from 907 to 910. *De Tribus Symbolis.* Nicolas was Pope from 858 to 867. The Creed itself was not admitted into the Liturgy at Rome till 1014, but then with the interpolated clause. Bona, quoted by Dr. Pusey, On the Clause, p. 66.

[r] Ἐκ τοῦ Πατρὸς ἐκπορευόμενον, καὶ ἐκ τοῦ Υἱοῦ λαμβανόμενον. See Epiphanius's Longer Creed, above, p. 81. Dr. Pusey quotes Theophylact and others of the Eastern Church, as acknowledging *the doctrine*, pp. 72 sqq.

[s] Pearson puts the case thus: "Although the addition of words to the formal Creed, without the consent, and against the protestation of the Oriental Church, be not justifiable, yet that which was added is nevertheless a certain truth, and may be so used in that Creed by them who believe the same to be a truth, so long as they pretend it not to be a definition of

The original Nicene Creed, it is said, is still adhered to by the Monophysite and Nestorian sects. But with these exceptions, grievous as is the schism which has rent the Church asunder, its two great branches have at least this in common, that setting aside the "Filioque" interpolation in the 8th Article, and the insertion of the "Deum ex Deo" in the 2nd, they still agree to confess the faith in the words of the Constantinopolitan Formulary. The Apostles' Creed and the Athanasian are Creeds of the West, the Constantinopolitan is the Creed of the Church Universal.

THE CONSTANTINOPOLITAN CREED.

Ἡ ἁγία Πίστις, ἣν ἐξέθεντο οἱ ἅγιοι πατέρες ῥύ συμφωνοῦσα τῇ ἁγίᾳ καὶ μεγάλῃ συνόδῳ τῇ ἐν Νικαίᾳ [t].

1. ΠΙΣΤΕΥΟΜΕΝ εἰς ἕνα Θεὸν Πατέρα παντοκράτορα,
ποιητὴν οὐρανοῦ καὶ γῆς, ὁρατῶν τε πάντων καὶ ἀοράτων·

2. Καὶ εἰς ἕνα Κύριον, Ἰησοῦν Χριστόν,
τὸν υἱὸν τοῦ Θεοῦ τὸν μονογενῆ,
τὸν ἐκ τοῦ Πατρὸς γεννηθέντα πρὸ πάντων τῶν αἰώνων,
Φῶς ἐκ Φωτός,
Θεὸν ἀληθινὸν ἐκ Θεοῦ ἀληθινοῦ,
γεννηθέντα οὐ ποιηθέντα,

that Council, but an addition or explication inserted, and condemn not those who, out of a greater respect to such synodical determination, will admit of no such insertions, nor speak any other language than the Scriptures and their Fathers spake" on Art. 8.   [t] Labbe, IV. col. 842.

ὁμοούσιον τῷ Πατρί·
δι' οὗ τὰ πάντα ἐγένετο·

3. Τὸν δι' ἡμᾶς τοὺς ἀνθρώπους καὶ διὰ τὴν ἡμετέραν σωτηρίαν
κατελθόντα ἐκ τῶν οὐρανῶν,
καὶ σαρκωθέντα
ἐκ Πνεύματος ἁγίου καὶ Μαρίας τῆς Παρθένου,
καὶ ἐνανθρωπήσαντα·

4. Σταυρωθέντα τε ὑπὲρ ἡμῶν ἐπὶ Ποντίου Πιλάτου,
καὶ παθόντα,
καὶ ταφέντα·

5. Καὶ ἀναστάντα τῇ τρίτῃ ἡμέρᾳ,
κατὰ τὰς γραφάς·

6. Καὶ ἀνελθόντα εἰς τοὺς οὐρανοὺς
καὶ καθεζόμενον ἐκ δεξιῶν τοῦ Πατρός,

7. Καὶ πάλιν ἐρχόμενον μετὰ δόξης
κρῖναι ζῶντας καὶ νεκρούς·
οὗ τῆς βασιλείας οὐκ ἔσται τέλος·

8. Καὶ εἰς τὸ Πνεῦμα τὸ Ἅγιον,
τὸ Κύριον,
καὶ τὸ ζωοποιόν,
τὸ ἐκ τοῦ Πατρὸς ἐκπορευόμενον,
τὸ σὺν Πατρὶ καὶ Υἱῷ συμπροσκυνούμενον καὶ συνδοξαζόμενον,
τὸ λαλῆσαν διὰ τῶν προφητῶν·

9. Εἰς μίαν ἁγίαν καθολικὴν καὶ ἀποστολικὴν Ἐκκλησίαν·

10. Ὁμολογοῦμεν ἓν βάπτισμα εἰς ἄφεσιν ἁμαρτιῶν·

11. Προσδοκῶμεν ἀνάστασιν νεκρῶν,
Καὶ ζωὴν τοῦ μέλλοντος αἰῶνος· ἀμήν.

II. INTERROGATIVE CREEDS.

Sir William Palmer, in his Origines Liturgicæ, chap. v. § 3, referring in a note to the Baptismal Service of the Apostolical Constitutions [a], says, that "the Profession of faith in the Eastern Churches has generally been made by the sponsor or the person to be baptized, not in the form of answers to questions, but by repeating the Creed after the Priest." St. Cyril of Alexandria, however (A.D. 430), in his Commentary on St. John xxi. 15-17, speaks of a triple interrogation in baptism, as though suggested by the threefold question addressed by our Lord to St. Peter, which would imply a threefold use.

The Creed employed would naturally be the Creed of the particular Church in which the baptism was being administered. But after the Council of Ephesus, 431, which forbade the use of any other Creed than that of Nicæa, the Nicene Creed became the only lawful formulary [x], or eventually, what came to be regarded simply as an enlarged edition of the Nicene, the Constantinopolitan.

The Creed used in St. Cyril of Jerusalem's time (347 or 348) in the Church of Jerusalem has been already referred to [y]. The candidate was asked *ei*

---

[a] For which see above, p. 70.

[x] The Greeks complain of the Western Church that she disregards the Decree of the Council of Ephesus in baptizing with her own Formulary instead of the Nicene. Whatever may be the modern custom, however, the use at least of the Nicæno-Constantinopolitan Creed continued for some time in some of the Western Churches. Instances may be seen in Martene, de Antiquis Eccl. Ritibus, I., II., xi. and xii.

[y] Above, p. 50.

πιστεύει εἰς τὸ ὄνομα τοῦ Πατρὸς, καὶ τοῦ Υἱοῦ, καὶ τοῦ ἁγίου Πνεύματος, on acknowledging which he was plunged three several times beneath the water.

The following is from a document which probably represents a form of the Apostolical Constitutions earlier and simpler than the Greek text with which we are familiar—a Coptic version, itself a translation made in the beginning of the present century from the Sahidic. It occurs in a Baptismal Service corresponding to the one contained in the 7th book of the Greek Constitutions, but differs from it in various particulars, in none more than in the Creeds which are to be said by the Catechumen about to be baptized. I give the whole of the passage as it stands[a]. An extract from the Greek Constitutions has been given above, page 72 :—

"And when the Presbyter has taken hold of each one of those who are about to receive baptism, let him command him to renounce, saying,

'I will renounce thee, Satan,
'And all thy service,
'And all thy works.'

"And when he has renounced all these, let him anoint him with the oil of exorcism, saying,

'Let every evil spirit depart from thee.'

"And let the bishop or the presbyter receive him thus unclothed to place him in the water of baptism.

"Also let the deacon go with him into the water, and let him say to him, helping him that he may say,

---

[a] The Apostolical Constitutions or Canons of the Apostles in Coptic, with an English Translation by Archdeacon Tattam, pp. 58 sqq.

1. 'I believe in the only true God, the Father Almighty,
2. And in the only-begotten Son, Jesus Christ, our Lord and Saviour,
8. And in the Holy Spirit, the Quickener,
   The Trinity of the same essence,
9. In the holy Catholic Church,
12. In the life everlasting. Amen.'

"And let him who receives baptism repeat after all these, 'I believe this.'

"And he who bestows it shall lay his hand upon the head of him who receives, dipping him three times, confessing these things each time.

"And afterwards let him say again,
2. 'Dost thou believe in our Lord Jesus Christ, the only Son of God the Father,
3. 'That He became man in a wonderful manner for us, in an incomprehensible unity, by His Holy Spirit, without the seed of man,
4. 'And that He was crucified for us under Pontius Pilate,
   'Died, of His own will, once, for our salvation,
5. 'Rose on the third day, loosing the bands of death,
6. 'Ascended up into heaven,
   Sat on the right hand of His good Father, on high,
7. 'And cometh again to judge the living and the dead, at His appearing and His kingdom?
8. 'And dost Thou believe in the Holy good Spirit and Quickener, who wholly purifieth?
9. 'In the holy Church?'

H

"Let him again say 'I believe.'

"And let them go up out of the water, and the Presbyter shall anoint him with holy anointing oil, in the Name of Jesus Christ. Thus he shall anoint every one of the rest, and clothe them as the rest, and they shall enter into the Church."

Then follows the Confirmation.

"Let the Bishop lay his hand upon them with affection, saying, Lord God, as Thou hast made these worthy to receive the forgiveness of their sins in the coming world, make them worthy to be filled with Thy Holy Spirit, and send upon them Thy grace, that they may serve Thee according to Thy will, for Thine is the glory, the Father, and the Son, and the Holy Spirit, in the Holy Church, now and always and for ever and ever. And he shall pour of the oil of thanksgiving in his hand, and put his hand upon his head, saying, 'I anoint thee with the holy anointing oil from God the Father, and Jesus Christ, and the Holy Spirit.' And he shall seal upon his forehead, saluting him. And he shall say, 'The Lord be with thee.' He who hath been sealed shall answer, 'And with Thy Spirit.'"

I add the following preparatory ceremonial, "Ad faciendum Catechumenum," from Goar's Εὐχολόγιον, p. 338.

After the usual renunciation of Satan, the Catechumen is asked, three several times, Συντάσσῃ τῷ Χριστῷ; to which he replies each time, Συντάσσομαι.' Once more the Priest asks, Συνετάξω τῷ Χριστῷ; and he again answers Συνεταξάμην. Then follows the question, Καὶ πιστεύεις αὐτῷ; to which he replies, Πιστεύω αὐτῷ, ὡς βασιλεῖ καὶ Θεῷ, and forthwith proceeds to rehearse the Creed, Πιστεύω εἰς ἕνα Θεὸν, κ.τ.λ. (either the Nicene or the Nicæno-Constantinopolitan Formulary). This he does three times, after which he is again asked, Συντάξω τῷ Χριστῷ; and again answers, Συνεταξάμην. Then the Priest says, Καὶ προσκυνήσον αὐτῷ, whereupon he prostrates himself, saying, Προσκυνῶ Πατέρα, Υἱόν, καὶ Ἅγιον Πνεῦμα, Τριάδα ὁμοούσιον καὶ ἀχώριστον.

CHAPTER IV.

THE DEFINITION OF FAITH OF THE COUNCIL OF CHALCEDON AND THE QUICUNQUE VULT, COMMONLY CALLED THE ATHANASIAN CREED.

Compellimur hæreticorum et blasphemantium vitiis illicita agere, ardua scandere, ineffabilia eloqui, inconcessa præsumere: et cum sola fide expleri quæ præcepta sunt oportet, adorare videlicet Patrem, et venerari cum Eo Filium, Sancto Spiritu abundare, cogimur sermonis nostri humilitatem ad ea quæ inenarribilia sunt extendere, et in vitium vitio coarctamur alieno, ut quæ contineri religione mentium oportuissent, nunc in periculum humani eloquii proferantur. Hilar. de Trinitate, ii. § 2.

CHAPTER IV.

THE DEFINITION OF FAITH OF THE COUNCIL OF CHALCEDON AND THE QUICUNQUE VULT, COMMONLY CALLED THE ATHANASIAN CREED.

The Definition of Faith of the Council of Chalcedon and the Quicunque Vult are enlarged Expositions of Christian doctrine made with special reference to certain Articles of the faith, with which heresy has tampered, rather than concise summaries, such as the Apostles' and Nicene Creeds. I place them therefore in a separate chapter.

I. THE DEFINITION OF FAITH OF THE COUNCIL OF CHALCEDON.

The Creed of Nicæa had been put forth as a safeguard against Arianism. It had been enlarged in the Constantinopolitan edition with an eye to the heresies of Apollinaris and Macedonius. The fifth century witnessed the rise of two new heresies, Nestorianism and Eutychianism.

Nestorius was a native of Germanicia, a town in the Patriarchate of Antioch, of which Church he became a Presbyter. But the See of Constantinople becoming vacant (A.D. 428), the Emperor Theodosius, who was determined that none of the Constantinopolitan clergy should succeed, sent for him, and caused him to be consecrated Bishop. His heresy was a recoil from Apollinarianism, in that branch of it which held that the Λόγος, the Divine Word, was to our blessed Lord what the soul is to ordinary men. Apollinarianism had extensively infected the Syrian Church of which Antioch was the metropolis, and the Antiochian Clergy, in their zeal against it, were led to lay much stress on the distinction between the divine and human natures in the Saviour, and in so doing sometimes to express themselves so unguardedly as to give occasion for the charge—possibly without sufficient foundation in the first instance, but afterwards justified by the position which in the heat of controversy they were driven to take—that they divided Christ into two persons, the Man Christ Jesus, and the Son of God, who had vouchsafed to unite Himself to that Man in the closest union (ἄκρα συνάφεια), dwelling in Him as in the Saints, only with a closer and more intimate indwelling. On this hypothesis the Son of God was one with the Son of Man, and the Son of Man was exalted to share the dignity and authority (ἀξία, αὐθεντία) of the Son of God, as a wife with her husband, but the Son of God had not actually become Man. It followed that He who was born of the blessed Virgin, though united to the Son of God in the closest and most intimate union, was not actually the Son of God, but Man only, and the blessed Virgin consequently ought not, in the language then coming extensively into vogue, to be called Θεοτόκος, " the Mother of God." "The Mother of Christ," Χριστοτόκος, she might be called, but not the " Mother of God."

It was this term Θεοτόκος which served as a spark to ignite the combustible materials which lay ready to explode. A Presbyter named Anastasius, whom Nestorius had brought with him from Antioch, and for whom he had a high regard, exclaimed one day while preaching, "Let no one call Mary Θεοτόκος, for Mary was but a woman, and for a woman to give birth to God is impossible." These words caused a great disturbance, many looking upon them as a denial of the Deity of our Lord, while at the same time they seemed to detract from the honour of His Mother.

Nestorius defended his Presbyter, and in his own sermons continued to reprobate the term. By and by the controversy was taken up by Cyril, Patriarch of Alexandria, two of whose letters in connexion with it came afterwards to be regarded as standards of orthodoxy [a].

Eventually, to determine the matter, the Emperor Theodosius was persuaded to summon a Council. This he did in his own name and that of the Western Emperor, appointing the place of meeting to be Ephesus, and the time, the following Whitsuntide, A.D. 431.

---

[a] The letters referred to in the text are the Second to Nestorius, and the Letters to John of Antioch. These are the Letters specified in the Definition of Faith of the Council of Chalcedon. They were both read and authoritatively sanctioned at the Council, as the former of them had been at Ephesus. Labbe, III. 462. A third Epistle, the one with the 12 anathemas appended, was read at Chalcedon, but it was not authoritatively sanctioned, the said anathemas being with many of the Fathers a ground of objection.

The Council met accordingly. It accepted the teaching of Cyril, as being in accordance with the Nicene Creed, and condemned that of Nestorius as impious and heretical. Nestorius was deposed, and was commanded by the Emperor to retire to a monastery near Antioch, of which he had formerly been an inmate. There he was suffered to remain nearly four years. But at length his enemies persuaded Theodosius to adopt severer measures. He was banished to the great Oasis, where he was captured by a wild tribe, and afterwards dismissed by them, as a prize not worth the trouble of taking charge of. He then surrendered himself into the hands of the Imperial Officers, by whom he was treated with great cruelty, and dragged about from place to place, till death put an end to his sufferings, about the year 440. Evagr. i. 7. Cyril died in 444.

Eutyches was the Archimandrite or Abbot of a monastery in the suburbs of Constantinople. He had taken a prominent part in opposing Nestorius, but became himself the author of another heresy at least as disastrous as Nestorius's. As Nestorius's heresy related to the Person of our blessed Lord, so that of Eutyches related to his Natures. Two Natures he acknowledged before the Incarnation, the Godhead and the Manhood. Afterwards he held that there was but one. The Human nature was absorbed by the Divine.

Flavian, Bishop of Constantinople, on hearing of his teaching, summoned him before a synod of bishops who, as it happened, were at Constantinople, on business of their own. His doctrine was condemned, and he was deprived of his office of Archimandrite, deposed from the Priesthood, and excommunicated. Labbe, III. 143.

On this he appealed to Leo, Bishop of Rome, complaining of the injustice with which he had been treated. Flavian also wrote to Leo, and received in reply the letter which is referred to in the following Definition of Faith, and is there sanctioned as a standard of orthodoxy on the subjects of which it treats.

Meanwhile the Emperor Theodosius, concerned at the state of things, summoned a Council to be held at Ephesus. The Council met on Aug. 10, 449, under the Presidency of Dioscorus, Patriarch of Alexandria. It reversed the decision of the Constantinopolitan Synod, acquitted Eutyches of heresy, and restored him to the priesthood and to his office. But its proceedings were of so outrageous a character that another Council became a necessity, and Leo besought the Emperor to convene one to be held in Italy. This Theodosius refused, but Marcian, his successor, on the request being repeated, acquiesced so far, as to grant that there should be a Council, but not that it should be held in Italy. The place first fixed upon was Nicæa; but this was afterwards changed for Chalcedon. The Council met accordingly in the autumn of 451, its first Session being held on Oct. 8.

The Council reversed the decisions of the Ephesine Council, the "Latrocinium" or "Robber Council," as it has been called from its outrageous proceedings, deposed Dioscorus, who had presided, and anathematized Eutyches and his heresy, and after much discussion [b], agreed upon a Definition or Declaration of the Faith, in which they embody the Creeds of Nicæa and Constantinople together with two of Cyril's Epistles and the Epistle of Leo to Flavian, and conclude with an explicit statement of the Catholic doctrine on those points on which it had been perverted by the heresies of Nestorius and Eutyches.

Of Eutyches after the Council hardly anything is known. An edict of the Emperor deposed him from the priesthood: but he appears to have returned to his Monastery,—of course not as Archimandrite. Among the Epistles of Leo there are two (Epp. 45 and 70), in which he intreats Marcian and Pulcheria to expel him from thence, and to send him into exile. But whether the intreaty was granted or refused is not known.

[b] See the account in Labbe, IV. coll. 555—561, and Evagrius ii. c. 18. When there seemed no prospect of agreement, reference was made to the Emperor, who sent word that unless some "Definition" be decided upon, another Council must be held in the West. At length the Imperial Commissioners, together with certain of the bishops, at the request of the whole Council, retired to the Oratory of the Church of St. Euphemia, in which the Council was being held, and on their return brought with them the "Definitio" on which they had agreed, which was then read aloud by the direction of the Commissioners, who describe it as τὰ ὁρισθέντα ἐπὶ παρουσίᾳ ἡμετέρᾳ παρὰ τῶν συνελθόντων ἁγίων πατέρων. cc. 559-61.

DEFINITIO FIDEI APUD CONCILIUM CHALCEDONENSE[e].

A.D. 451.

Ἡ ἉΓΙΑ καὶ μεγάλη καὶ οἰκουμενικὴ Σύνοδος, ἡ κατὰ Θεοῦ χάριν καὶ θέσπισμα τῶν εὐσεβεστάτων καὶ φιλοχρίστων ἡμῶν Βασιλέων, Μαρκιανοῦ[d] καὶ Οὐαλεντινιανοῦ[e] Αὐγούστων, συναχθεῖσα ἐν τῇ Καλχηδονέων μητροπόλει[f] τῆς Βιθυνῶν ἐπαρχίας, ἐν τῷ μαρτυρίῳ τῆς ἁγίας καὶ καλλινίκου μάρτυρος Εὐφημίας, ὥρισε τὰ ὑποτεταγμένα·

Ὁ ΚΥΡΙΟΣ ἡμῶν καὶ Σωτήρ, Ἰησοῦς Χριστός, τῆς πίστεως τὴν γνῶσιν τοῖς μαθηταῖς βεβαιῶν, ἔφη· ' Εἰρήνην τὴν ἐμὴν ἀφίημι ὑμῖν, εἰρήνην τὴν ἐμὴν δίδωμι ὑμῖν·' ὥστε μηδένα πρὸς τὸν πλησίον διαφωνεῖν ἐν τοῖς δόγμασι τῆς εὐσεβείας, ἀλλ' ἐπίσης ἅπασι τὸ τῆς ἀληθείας ἐπιδείκνυσθαι κήρυγμα. Ἐπειδὴ δὲ οὐ παύεται διὰ τῶν ἑαυτοῦ ζιζανίων ὁ πονηρὸς τοῖς τῆς εὐσεβείας ἐπιφυόμενος σπέρμασι, καί τι καινὸν κατὰ τῆς ἀληθείας ἐφευρίσκων ἀεί, διὰ τοῦτο συνήθως ὁ Δεσπότης προνοούμενος τοῦ ἀνθρωπίνου γένους, τὸν εὐσεβῆ τοῦτον καὶ πιστότατον πρὸς ζῆλον ἀνέστησε βασιλέα, καὶ τοὺς ἁπανταχῇ τῆς ἱερωσύνης πρὸς ἑαυτὸν ἀρχηγοὺς συνεκάλεσεν, ὥστε, τῆς χάριτος τοῦ πάντων ἡμῶν Δεσπότου Χριστοῦ ἐνεργούσης, πᾶσαν μὲν τοῦ ψεύδους τῶν τοῦ Χριστοῦ προβάτων ἀποσείσασθαι λύμην, τοῖς δὲ τῆς ἀληθείας αὐτὰ καταπιαίνειν βλα-

---

[e] Labbe, IV. c. 562, sqq.
[d] Emperor of the East.   [e] Emperor of the West.
[f] Chalcedon, in the 6th Session, for the honour of the holy martyr, Euphemia, in whose Church the Council was being held, and for the honour of the Council, was raised by the Emperor to the nominal rank of a metropolis, Bithynia, the original metropolis, still retaining its place. Labbe, IV. c. 611.

στήμασιν. Ὁ δὴ καὶ πεποιήκαμεν, κοινῇ ψήφῳ τὰ τῆς πλάνης ἀπελάσαντες δόγματα, τὴν δὲ ἀπλανῆ τῶν Πατέρων ἀνανεωσάμενοι πίστιν, τὸ τῶν τριακοσίων δεκαοκτὼ σύμβολον[e] τοῖς πᾶσι κηρύξαντες, καὶ ὡς οἰκείους τοὺς τοῦτο τὸ σύνθεμα τῆς εὐσεβείας δεξαμένους Πατέρας ἐπιγραψάμενοι, οἵπερ εἰσὶν οἱ μετὰ ταῦτα ἐν τῇ μεγάλῃ Κωνσταντινουπόλει συνελθόντες ρν', καὶ αὐτοὶ τὴν αὐτὴν ἐπισφραγισάμενοι πίστιν. Ὁρίζομεν τοίνυν, (τὴν τάξιν καὶ τοὺς περὶ τῆς πίστεως ἅπαντας τύπους φυλάττοντες καὶ ἡμεῖς τῆς κατ' Ἔφεσον πάλαι γεγενημένης ἁγίας Συνόδου, ἧς ἡγεμόνες οἱ ἁγιώτατοι τὴν μνήμην Κελεστῖνος, ὁ τῆς Ῥωμαίων, καὶ Κύριλλος, ὁ τῆς Ἀλεξανδρέων, ἐτύγχανον,) προλάμπειν μὲν τῆς ὀρθῆς καὶ ἀμωμήτου πίστεως τὴν ἔκθεσιν τῶν τιη' ἁγίων καὶ μακαρίων Πατέρων τῶν ἐν Νικαίᾳ, ἐπὶ τοῦ εὐσεβοῦς μνήμης Κωνσταντίνου τοῦ γενομένου Βασιλέως, συναχθέντων· κρατεῖν δὲ καὶ τὰ παρὰ τῶν ρν' ἁγίων Πατέρων ἐν Κωνσταντινουπόλει ὁρισθέντα, πρὸς ἀναίρεσιν μὲν τῶν τότε φυεισῶν αἱρέσεων, βεβαίωσιν δὲ τῆς αὐτῆς καθολικῆς καὶ ἀποστολικῆς ἡμῶν πίστεως.

Σύμβολον τῶν ἐν Νικαίᾳ τιη'.

Πιστεύομεν εἰς ἕνα Θεόν, Πατέρα παντοκράτορα, πάντων ὁρατῶν τε καὶ ἀοράτων ποιητήν· καὶ εἰς ἕνα Κύριον Ἰησοῦν Χριστόν, τὸν υἱὸν τοῦ Θεοῦ, τὸν γεννηθέντα ἐκ τοῦ Πατρὸς μονογενῆ, τουτέστιν, ἐκ τῆς οὐσίας τοῦ Πατρός, Θεὸν ἐκ Θεοῦ, φῶς ἐκ φωτός, Θεὸν ἀληθινὸν ἐκ Θεοῦ ἀληθινοῦ, γεννηθέντα οὐ ποιηθέντα, ὁμοούσιον τῷ Πατρί, δι' οὗ τὰ πάντα ἐγένετο· τόν, δι' ἡμᾶς τοὺς ἀνθρώπους καὶ διὰ τὴν ἡμετέραν σωτηρίαν, κατελθόντα ἐκ τῶν οὐράνων, καὶ σαρκωθέντα ἐκ Πνεύματος ἁγίου καὶ Μαρίας τῆς Παρθένου, καὶ ἐνανθρωπήσαντα, σταυ-

[e] Four different words, it will be observed, are used for a Confession of Faith in this document, σύμβολον, σύνθεμα πίστις, ἔκθεσις. It is itself called Ὅρος.

ρωθέντα τε ὑπὲρ ἡμῶν ἐπὶ Ποντίου Πιλάτου, καὶ παθόντα, καὶ ταφέντα, καὶ ἀναστάντα τῇ τρίτῃ ἡμέρᾳ κατὰ τὰς γραφάς, καὶ ἀνελθόντα εἰς τοὺς οὐρανούς, καὶ καθεζόμενον ἐν δεξιᾷ τοῦ Πατρός, καὶ πάλιν ἐρχόμενον μετὰ δόξης κρῖναι ζῶντας καὶ νεκρούς, οὗ τῆς Βασιλείας οὐκ ἔσται τέλος· καὶ εἰς τὸ Πνεῦμα τὸ ἅγιον, τὸ κύριον, τὸ ζωοποιόν. Τοὺς δὲ λέγοντας, ἦν ποτε ὅτε οὐκ ἦν, καὶ πρὶν γεννηθῆναι οὐκ ἦν, καὶ ὅτι ἐξ οὐκ ὄντων ἐγένετο, ἢ ἐξ ἑτέρας ὑποστάσεως ἢ οὐσίας φάσκοντας εἶναι, ἢ τρεπτὸν, ἢ ἀλλοιωτὸν τὸν Υἱὸν τοῦ Θεοῦ, τούτους ἀναθεματίζει ἡ καθολικὴ καὶ ἀποστολικὴ ἐκκλησία.

The above is here given in full, since it varies from the original Nicene Creed at p. 58 above, as recited at the 2nd Session.

Then follows the Constantinopolitan Creed, τὸ τῶν ρν' ἁγίων πατέρων σύμβολον τῶν ἐν Κωνσταντινουπόλει συναχθέντων, which is identical with the Constantinopolitan Creed at p. 75.

Ἤρκει μὲν οὖν εἰς ἐντελῆ τῆς εὐσεβείας ἐπίγνωσίν τε καὶ βεβαίωσιν τὸ σοφὸν καὶ σωτήριον τοῦτο τῆς θείας χάριτος σύμβολον· Περί τε γὰρ τοῦ Πατρὸς καὶ τοῦ Υἱοῦ καὶ τοῦ Ἁγίου Πνεύματος ἐκδιδάσκει τὸ τέλειον, καὶ τοῦ Κυρίου τὴν ἐνανθρώπησιν τοῖς πιστῶς δεχομένοις παρίστησιν. Ἀλλ' ἐπειδήπερ οἱ τῆς ἀληθείας ἀθετεῖν ἐπιχειροῦντες τὸ κήρυγμα διὰ τῶν οἰκείων αἱρέσεων τὰς κενοφωνίας ἀπέτεκον, οἱ μὲν τὸ τῆς δι' ἡμᾶς τοῦ Κυρίου οἰκονομίας[b] μυστήριον παραφθείρειν

[b] Οἰκονομία, "Dispensation." The word came to be applied more especially to the *Incarnation*, because this was *par excellence* the plan which God had ordained for the government of His household. Hence in the province of Theology, οἰκονομία was distinguished by the Fathers from Θεολογία proper, the former being the teaching which was concerned

τολμῶντες, καὶ τὴν "Θεοτόκον" ἐπὶ τῆς Παρθένου φωνὴν ἀπαρνούμενοι, οἱ δὲ σύγχυσιν καὶ κρᾶσιν εἰσάγοντες, καὶ μίαν εἶναι φύσιν τῆς σαρκὸς καὶ τῆς Θεότητος ἀνοήτως ἀναπλάττοντες, καὶ παθητὴν τοῦ Μονογενοῦς τὴν θείαν φύσιν τῇ συγχύσει τερατευόμενοι, διὰ τοῦτο πᾶσαν αὐτοῖς ἀποκλεῖσαι κατὰ τῆς ἀληθείας μηχανὴν βουλομένη ἡ παροῦσα νῦν αὕτη ἁγία μεγάλη καὶ οἰκουμενικὴ Σύνοδος, τὸ τοῦ κηρύγματος ἄνωθεν ἀσάλευτον ἐκδιδάσκουσα, ὥρισε προηγουμένως, τῶν τριακοσίων δεκαοκτὼ ἁγίων Πατέρων τὴν πίστιν μένειν ἀπαρεγχείρητον, καὶ διὰ μὲν τοὺς τῷ Πνεύματι τῷ Ἁγίῳ μαχομένους, τὴν χρόνοις ὕστερον παρὰ τῶν ἐπὶ τῆς βασιλευούσης πόλεως συνελθόντων ἑκατὸν πεντήκοντα ἁγίων Πατέρων περὶ τῆς τοῦ Πνεύματος οὐσίας παραδοθεῖσαν διδασκαλίαν κυροῖ, ἣν ἐκεῖνοι τοῖς πᾶσιν ἐγνώρισαν, οὐκ ὥς τι λεῖπον τοῖς προλαβοῦσιν ἐπάγοντες, ἀλλὰ τὴν περὶ τοῦ Ἁγίου Πνεύματος αὐτῶν ἔννοιαν κατὰ τῶν τὴν αὐτοῦ δεσποτείαν ἀθετεῖν πειρωμένων γραφικαῖς μαρτυρίαις τρανώσαντες[1]. Διὰ δὲ τοὺς τὸ τῆς οἰκονομίας παραφθείρειν ἐπιχειροῦντας μυστήριον, καὶ ψιλὸν ἄνθρωπον εἶναι τὸν ἐκ τῆς ἁγίας τεχθέντα Μαρίας ἀναιδῶς ληρῳδοῦντας, τὰς τοῦ μακαρίου Κυρίλλου, τοῦ τῆς Ἀλεξανδρέων Ἐκκλησίας γενομένου ποιμένος, συνοδικὰς ἐπιστολὰς πρὸς Νεστόριον καὶ πρὸς τοὺς τῆς ἀνατολῆς [k], ἁρμοδίους οὔσας, ἐδέξατο, εἰς ἔλεγχον μὲν τῆς Νεστορίου φρενοβλαβείας, ἑρμηνείαν δὲ τῶν ἐν εὐσεβεῖ ζήλῳ τοῦ σωτηρίου συμβόλου ποθούντων τὴν ἔννοιαν· αἷς καὶ τὴν ἐπιστολὴν τοῦ

with the Incarnation and its consequences, the latter the teaching which related to the eternal and divine nature of Christ. Bp. Lightfoot, Ignat., p. 75.

Glancing at the Decree of the Council of Ephesus, which forbade the making of additions to the Creed of Nicæa.

[k] St. Cyril's 2nd Epistle to Nestorius and his Epistle to John of Antioch.

τῆς μεγίστης καὶ πρεσβυτέρας Ῥώμης προέδρου, τοῦ μακαριωτάτου καὶ ἁγιωτάτου Ἀρχιεπισκόπου Λέοντος, τὴν γραφεῖσαν πρὸς τὸν ἐν ἁγίοις Ἀρχιεπίσκοπον Φλαυιανὸν, ἐπ' ἀναιρέσει τῆς Εὐτυχοῦς κακονοίας, ἅτε δὴ τῇ τοῦ μεγάλου Πέτρου ὁμολογίᾳ συμβαίνουσαν, καὶ κοινήν τινα στήλην ὑπάρχουσαν κατὰ τῶν κακοδοξούντων, εἰκότως συνήρμοσε πρὸς τὴν τῶν ὀρθοδόξων δογμάτων βεβαίωσιν. Τοῖς τε γὰρ εἰς υἱῶν δυάδα τὸ τῆς οἰκονομίας διασπᾶν ἐπιχειροῦσι μυστήριον παρατάττεται, καὶ τοὺς παθητὴν τοῦ Μονογενοῦς λέγειν τολμῶντας τὴν Θεότητα τοῦ τῶν ἱερῶν ἀπωθεῖται συλλόγου, καὶ τοῖς ἐπὶ τῶν δύο φύσεων τοῦ Χριστοῦ κρᾶσιν ἢ σύγχυσιν ἐπινοοῦσιν ἀνθίσταται, καὶ τοὺς οὐρανίου ἢ ἑτέρας τινὸς ὑπάρχειν οὐσίας τὴν ἐξ ἡμῶν ληφθεῖσαν αὐτῷ τοῦ δούλου μορφὴν παραπαίοντας ἐξελαύνει, καὶ τοὺς δύο μὲν πρὸ τῆς ἑνώσεως φύσεις τοῦ Κυρίου μυθεύοντας, μίαν δὲ μετὰ τὴν ἕνωσιν ἀναπλάττοντας ἀναθεματίζει.

ΕΠΟΜΕΝΟΙ τοίνυν τοῖς ἁγίοις Πατράσιν, ἕνα καὶ τὸν αὐτὸν ὁμολογοῦμεν Υἱὸν τὸν Κύριον ἡμῶν, Ἰησοῦν Χριστόν, καὶ συμφώνως ἅπαντες ἐκδιδάσκομεν, τέλειον τὸν αὐτὸν ἐν Θεότητι, τέλειον τὸν αὐτὸν ἐν ἀνθρωπότητι, Θεὸν ἀληθῶς, καὶ ἄνθρωπον ἀληθῶς, τὸν αὐτὸν ἐκ ψυχῆς λογικῆς καὶ σώματος, ὁμοούσιον τῷ Πατρὶ κατὰ τὴν Θεότητα, καὶ ὁμοούσιον τὸν αὐτὸν ἡμῖν κατὰ τὴν ἀνθρωπότητα, κατὰ πάντα ὅμοιον ἡμῖν χωρὶς ἁμαρτίας, πρὸ αἰώνων μὲν ἐκ τοῦ Πατρὸς γεννηθέντα κατὰ τὴν Θεότητα, ἐπ' ἐσχάτων δὲ τῶν ἡμερῶν τὸν αὐτὸν, δι' ἡμᾶς καὶ διὰ τὴν ἡμετέραν σωτηρίαν, ἐκ Μαρίας τῆς Παρθένου τῆς Θεοτόκου κατὰ τὴν ἀνθρωπότητα, ἕνα καὶ τὸν αὐτὸν Χριστόν, Υἱόν, Κύριον, μονογενῆ, ἐν[1] δύο φύσεσιν ἀσυγχύτως,

---

[1] The Greek text, as it stands in the record of the Council, is ἐκ δύο φύσεων. On the reading see Routh, Opusc. ii. p. 119. Héfélé, iii. p. 68, French translation. Dr. Routh conjectures

ἀτρέπτως, ἀδιαιρέτως, ἀχωρίστως γνωριζόμενον, οὐδαμοῦ τῆς τῶν φύσεων διαφορᾶς ἀνῃρημένης διὰ τὴν ἕνωσιν, σωζομένης δὲ μᾶλλον τῆς ἰδιότητος ἑκατέρας φύσεως, καὶ εἰς ἓν πρόσωπον καὶ μίαν ὑπόστασιν συντρεχούσης, οὐχ ὡς εἰς δύο πρόσωπα μεριζόμενον ἢ διαιρούμενον, ἀλλ' ἕνα καὶ τὸν αὐτὸν Υἱὸν καὶ μονογενῆ Θεόν, Λόγον, Κύριον, Ἰησοῦν Χριστόν· καθάπερ ἄνωθεν οἱ Προφῆται περὶ αὐτοῦ, καὶ αὐτὸς ἡμᾶς ὁ Κύριος, Ἰησοῦς Χριστός, ἐξεπαίδευσε, καὶ τὸ τῶν Πατέρων ἡμῖν παραδέδωκε σύμβολον.

Τούτων τοίνυν μετὰ πάσης πανταχόθεν ἀκριβείας τε καὶ ἐμμελείας παρ' ἡμῶν διατυπωθέντων, ὥρισεν ἡ ἁγία καὶ οἰκουμενικὴ Σύνοδος, ἑτέραν πίστιν μηδενὶ ἐξεῖναι προφέρειν, ἤγουν συγγράφειν, ἢ συντιθέναι, ἢ φρονεῖν, ἢ διδάσκειν ἑτέρους· τοὺς δὲ τολμῶντας ἢ συντιθέναι πίστιν ἑτέραν, ἤγουν προκομίζειν, ἢ διδάσκειν, ἢ παραδιδόναι ἕτερον σύμβολον [m] τοῖς ἐθέλουσιν ἐπιστρέφειν εἰς ἐπίγνωσιν ἀληθείας ἐξ Ἑλληνισμοῦ, ἢ ἐξ Ἰουδαϊσμοῦ, ἤγουν ἐξ αἱρέσεως οἱασδηποτοῦν, τούτους, εἰ μὲν εἶεν Ἐπίσκοποι ἢ κληρικοί, ἀλλοτρίους εἶναι τοὺς Ἐπισκόπους τῆς ἐπισκοπῆς, καὶ τοὺς κληρικοὺς τοῦ κλήρου· εἰ δὲ μονάζοντες ἢ λαϊκοὶ εἶεν, ἀναθεματίζεσθαι αὐτούς [n].

that the original was ἐκ δύο φύσεων καὶ ἐν δύο φύσεσιν, which certainly is more in keeping with the mind of the Council.

[m] The Council seem to imply that the Nicene and Constantinopolitan Creeds, both of which they have just recited, are virtually one.

[n] See the 7th Canon of the Council of Ephesus, which the "Definition" here repeats almost to the letter.

The Church of Rome, by its additions to the Creed of Constantinople in the Creed of Pope Pius IV., has presumed to set at nought these decrees of two General Councils.

II. THE QUICUNQUE VULT, COMMONLY CALLED THE ATHANASIAN CREED[a].

EVERYTHING relating to the History of the Athanasian Creed is involved in obscurity.

The earliest writer who appears to have done anything towards the investigation of the subject was Gerrard Vossius, who, in his Dissertation "De Tribus Symbolis," published in 1642, ascribed it to the 8th or 9th century. In a later work, published after his death, he carried its age back to about the year 600, having been influenced by the opinion of Archbishop Ussher. Ussher had met with a manuscript Psalter, in the Library of Sir Robert Cotton, which contained the Creed, and which, from the character of the hand-writing, he conjectured to be of that date. Bishop Pearson, in his Exposition of the Creed, published in 1659, expresses the same opinion, though on another ground[b].

Various other writers, almost all of them foreigners, bestowed more or less attention on the subject. But the writer, whose work till of late was accepted in this country as the most complete and exhaustive, was Waterland. In his *Critical History of the Athanasian Creed*, published in 1727, Waterland collected together all that had been contributed by preceding

---

[a] Much of this chapter is from a Review of *Dr. Swainson's* Work on the Creeds, contributed by the author to the *Christian Observer*, March, 1875.

[b] "Though we cannot say it was Athanasius's, yet we know it was extant about the year 600, by the Epistle of *Isidorus Hispalensis ad Claudium Ducem*." On Art. 5.

writers; and the conclusion to which he came was, that the Creed must have been written about the year 430, that the country to which it owed its birth was Gaul, that the language in which it was originally written was Latin, and that its author was Hilary, Bishop of Arles.

Waterland's book seemed to have set the question at rest, and its conclusions were pretty generally acquiesced in till a few years ago, when Mr. Ffoulkes reopened the subject, imagining that he had discovered the long-sought author of the Creed in Paulinus, Patriarch of Aquileia, and asserted that the date could not be placed earlier than about the year 800.

Mr. Ffoulkes' hypothesis was extremely popular when first proposed, and was welcomed by many who had no liking for the Creed, and were glad of an argument which seemed to detract from its authority. Its practical result was to reopen the investigation. Various writers have since entered the field, fresh researches have been made, Libraries have been ransacked for manuscripts, considerations not before thought of have been suggested, yet when all has been done, it is doubtful whether the question has been brought nearer to solution than before. Of the writers referred to, those whose names stand in the forefront are the late Dr. Swainson, Lady Margaret's Professor of Divinity at Cambridge [c],

---

[c] *The Nicene and Apostles' Creeds, their Literary History, together with an account of the Growth and Reception of the Sermon on the Faith, commonly called The Creed of St. Athanasius.* London, Murray, 1875.

Dr. Lumby[d], Norrisian Professor, and Mr. Ommanney[e].

The conclusion at which Dr. Swainson arrives is, that though portions of the Creed may have existed at an earlier period, yet as a whole "it was not known in its present form before the latter years of the eighth century" (p. 195). With obvious inconsistency, towards the close of his book (p. 448), he removes the date somewhat approaching to a century later,—to "between the years 860 or 870."

Dr. Lumby agrees with Dr. Swainson as to the composite character of the work; but dates the combination of the separate parts at some time between A.D. 800 and 825 (p. 252).

Mr. Ommanney, rejecting the composite theory, produces evidence of the existence of the Quicunque in its entirety antecedently to the 9th century. And he shews that there is good reason for believing, that it may be traced as far back as to the end— probably even to the middle—of the fifth century.

My own belief, arrived at some years before the publication of the earliest of the beforementioned works, but confirmed by the statements contained in them, is, that even on external grounds, we have good reasons for assigning the Quicunque to a date at least as early as the middle of the 7th century, if

---

[d] *The History of the Creeds*, by J. Rawson Lumby, B.D. Cambridge and London, 1873.

[e] *Early History of the Athanasian Creed.* London, Rivingtons, 1880. *The Athanasian Creed, an Examination of recent theories respecting its Age and Origin.* London, Rivingtons, 1875. *The S.P.C.K. and the Creed of St. Athanasius.*

not earlier. Internal considerations make it probable that it should be assigned to a date as early as that to which Mr. Ommanney would refer it.

As to the composite theory, it has too much the appearance of having been resorted to in order to support a conclusion already determined upon. The Quicunque is a natural whole, in which the several parts fit naturally into their respective places. It is in fact neither more nor less than the Apostles' Creed, with those articles enlarged which relate to the Trinity and the Incarnation,—I., II., VIII., III.,—those great articles in the guarding of which from the perversions of heresy the Church's earliest conflicts were engaged, the other articles remaining for the most part as they stand in the original. Separate the portions which are supposed to have been originally separate, and either portion is obviously incomplete.

i. EXTERNAL EVIDENCE AS TO DATE.

1. The earliest MS. to which Waterland refers is a Psalter which Archbishop Ussher had met with in the Library of Sir Robert Cotton, but which, when Waterland wrote, was nowhere to be found. Ussher conjectured it to have been written about the year 600. In describing its contents, however, he mentioned that among them there was a copy of the Apostles' Creed, complete in all its parts, such as it was in his own day. This circumstance led me to doubt whether Ussher had not placed the date of the MS. too early, for there is, so far as I am aware, no

extant instance of such completeness so early as the year 600[e].

Ussher rested his opinion upon the character of the hand-writing. The discovery of the missing manuscript[f] some few years since has enabled modern experts in palæography to form their own judgment on that point. It had found its way by some means into the public Library at Utrecht. And the authorities with great liberality permitted it to be brought to England for a time, and placed in the British Museum for the inspection of such persons as might be interested in the matter. They went further. They permitted it to be photographed, and a considerable number of copies were taken.

The almost universal opinion of competent judges who have seen the MS. since its discovery, or the photograph, is that Archbishop Ussher was mistaken,

---

[e] The reader is referred to a Pamphlet, published in 1872, some time before the discovery of the Utrecht Psalter, entitled, *The Athanasian Creed,—Reasons for rejecting Mr. Ffoulkes's Theory, as to its age and author.* Parker, Oxford.

[f] The discovery was due to Dr. Swainson, who was indebted for the suggestion which led to it to Professor Westwood, who had given a fac-simile of the hand-writing, with some account of the manuscript, in his Work on the *Miniatures and Ornaments of Anglo-Saxon and Irish Manuscripts.* Dr. Swainson gives an interesting account of the discovery, *History of the Creeds*, p. 197.

The MS. appears to have been given to the Library by a M. de Ridder in 1718: but who M. de Ridder was, or how he came by it, is not known. The Cotton Library perished by fire in 1731, so that the loss of the MS. to this country proved its preservation.

and that the date of the MS. ought not to be placed earlier than the early part of the ninth century.

The Creed itself, however, must be referred to an earlier date, for it is placed at the end of the Psalter with the Hymns of the Church, and in immediate sequence to the Lord's Prayer and the Apostles' Creed, a position which would not have been assigned to it unless it had already been in repute, and had already been of some age.

2. Another MS. referred to by Waterland would be of special importance if its reputed date were not open to question. This is the famous Golden Psalter in the Imperial Library at Vienna, which, on the authority of a copy of Latin verses on the first leaf, in which Charles, King of France, presents the MS. to Adrian on his election to the Papal Chair, Waterland, following Lambecius, assigns to the year 772, taking it for granted, that "Rex Carolus" means Charlemagne, and "Hadrianus," Adrian the 1st. Other circumstances, however, throw doubt upon the supposition, and it has been suggested that "Rex Carolus" may have been Charles the Bald, who reigned 840—877, and Pope Hadrian, Adrian the 2nd, who became Pope in 867[g].

Whatever uncertainty, however, may attach to the date of these manuscripts, we have sufficient evidence of the existence of the Creed at the beginning of the ninth century. Setting out from that point

---

[g] See the objections urged by Dr. Lumby, after Mr. Ffoulkes, *History of the Creeds*, p. 221. In a note Dr. L. gives a copy of the verses.

we can trace it step by step backward for at least a century and a half.

3. In the year 809, certain Latin monks, who were established in a convent at Jerusalem, and who had been subjected to ill-usage for reciting the Nicene Creed with the Filioque clause, vindicate themselves in a Letter to Pope Leo the 3rd, by appealing to the " Faith of Athanasius," among other documents, as likewise affirming the procession from the Son.

A doubt indeed has been suggested, whether the title, "The Faith of Athanasius," really meant the Quicunque, for it appears to have been given to other documents also: but the reference to the Procession from the Son, especially taken in connexion with the proof, presently to be produced, of the existence of the Creed at this time, confirms the supposition that it was the veritable Athanasian Creed that was meant.

4. A few years earlier—A.D. 798—we meet with a considerable portion of the Creed in a confession of his faith which Denebert, Bishop of Worcester, according to the custom of his time, exhibited on his consecration. "I will expound in few words," he says, "the Orthodox Catholic and Apostolic faith, as I have learnt it, because it is written [h], 'Whosoever would be saved, before all things it is necessary that he hold the Catholic faith.'" He then proceeds, in the precise words of our present Formulary, to the end of

---

[h] "This document is the more valuable because it proves that what is given is quoted from a *written* original—' Scriptum est.' "—Dr. Lumby, p. 228.

verse 6, after which, omitting verses 7—20, he continues to the end of that part of the Creed which relates to the Trinity. There is no ground for supposing that Denebert was ignorant of the remaining portion: his omission of it may have been due simply to the fact that it did not come within his purpose to recite it[i]. That the Creed existed at this time, and existed as a whole, we have evidence in two manuscripts which contain it in its entirety discovered by Mr. Ommanney in the Bibliothèque Nationale at Paris, both of which were written between the death of Pope Adrian I. at Christmas, 795, and the Coronation of Charlemagne as Emperor at Christmas, 800[k].

5. There is in the Bodleian Library a Manuscript (Junius 25) which contains a Commentary on the Athanasian Creed, ascribed by Waterland, after Muratori, though without sufficient reason, to Venantius Fortunatus. Seven other manuscripts containing this Commentary are known to exist[l]; but the Bodleian is supposed to be the oldest. From the character of the handwriting the late Librarian, Mr. Coxe, assigned it to the early part of the ninth century.

Whatever the age of the Manuscript, however,

---

[i] The passage is given in full by Dr. Swainson, p. 285, from Haddan and Stubbs' *Councils and Ecclesiastical Documents*.

[k] *Early History of the Athanasian Creed*, pp. 174 sqq., and 181 sqq.

[l] See Mr. Ommanney's account of them, pp. 47 sqq. Three of these were discovered by himself, two by Rev. W. D. Macray, Rector of Ducklington, Oxon.

there is strong internal evidence in the work itself
that it was composed before the close of the eighth
century; indeed, for anything that appears to the
contrary, it may have been composed very considerably before. Commenting on the clause, in verse 31,
" Man, of the substance of his mother, born in the
world (in sæculo)," the writer observes, " that is, in
this sixth millenary in which we now live," from
which the inference is obvious, that the Commentary
must have been written at some time,—it may have
been a long time,—before Anno Mundi 6000, and
this, adjusted to the Christian era, and estimated by
the Chronology current in the Middle Ages, would
coincide with A.D. 800 [m].

In confirmation of the supposition of a much
earlier date, it may be mentioned that the Commentary makes no reference to any heresy later than
the Apollinarian, though there are passages in the
Creed which, if the Commentary had been written
after the rise of Nestorianism and Eutychianism, in
the fifth century, would have made reference to those
heresies by the commentator almost unavoidable.

However, whatever the date of the Commentary,
even though it was composed as late as 800, we must
go back some considerable time for the date of the

---

[m] The reasons for this conclusion are stated in the writer's pamphlet, *The Athanasian Creed. Reasons for rejecting Mr. Ffoulkes' Theory as to its age and author.*

The reader may see what has been urged against the conclusion by Dr. Swainson, pp. 432—435, and what in confirmation of it by Mr. Ommanney, *History of the Athanasian Creed*,
pp. 150—153.

Creed commented upon. Documents of this sort do not gain sufficient repute to be made the subjects of a Commentary till they have been some years before the public. We may safely then, on the evidence thus far adduced, assume that the Creed must have been in existence at least as early as the middle, or even the earlier part, of the eighth century: it may have been, for anything that appears to the contrary, very much earlier.

6. Of its existence, and that in its entirety, at some time in that century, we have proof in a manuscript now in the Ambrosian Library at Milan, which Muratori, writing in 1698, supposed to be then about a thousand years old. Montfaucon and the present Librarian, Dr. Ceriani, without attempting to be more precise, simply assign it to the eighth century[n]. Waterland, following Muratori, places it, "to make a round number, at 700[o]."

7. We come at length to what I conceive to be the earliest external evidence at present accessible. There is, in the Bibliothèque Nationale at Paris, among the Colbert MSS., a Manuscript (No. 3836), which is generally allowed to belong to the earlier part of the eighth century, probably about 730[p].

---

[n] Dr. Swainson, pp. 317, 322.

[o] Waterland's Works, vol. iii. p. 150. Oxford, 1843.

[p] "I believe that the opinion is now nearly uniform, that the MS. was written about 730." *Swainson*, p. 262. By the kindness of the Librarian I was permitted to have photographs taken of the two pages on which the Creed is written. These the Palæographical Society have since reproduced and published in autotype.

This MS. contains a transcript from another and older manuscript, apparently, from its mutilated condition, considerably older. The transcriber prefaces his extract with the notice:—" This I found at Treves, in a manuscript beginning, 'Domini Nostri Jesu Christi et reliqua. Domini Nostri Jesu Christi fideliter credat,'" and then, taking up the words which follow, "Est ergo fides recta ut credamus et confitemur quia Dominus Jesus Christus, Dei Filius, Deus pariter et Homo est," proceeds to give the remaining words, not strictly indeed of the Creed, but of what would seem to be a sermon or address in which the Creed is incorporated, for the most part word for word, but yet with some variations more or less important. This of course implies a still earlier date of the Creed, portions of which are so incorporated.

The original MS. then from which the Paris MS. was transcribed, judging from the mutilated condition in which the transcriber seems to have found it, was in all probability of some age when the transcript was made. Are we asking too large an allowance if we suppose it some fifty or sixty years old? On this supposition its date would be about 680 or 670, at the latest.

And of this date there is a very striking confirmation in the document itself. For while every other verse of the corresponding portion of the Quicunque is represented in it, one verse—the verse containing the illustration "As the reasonable soul and flesh is one man, so God and man is one Christ,"—is conspicuous by its absence. It has been left out, and without question designedly left out; and no reason for the omission so likely as the apprehension of the use which the Eutychians were accustomed to make of it in their controversy with the Catholics. Now we have distinct proof of the extensive prevalence of Eutychianism at the time referred to. For Bede mentions this as the occasion of the assembling of the great synod of Hethfeld, and mentions it in such terms as to imply that it was one of the pressing dangers of the day, to which the Church generally—not merely the English branch of it—was exposed. The date of the synod of Hethfeld is 680 [q].

But the document, as I have said, is not the Quicunque itself, but a sermon or address—probably an address *in Traditione Symboli*—in which the words of the Quicunque are incorporated. Whatever the date, therefore, of the MS. which contains the document, we must go farther back for the date of the Quicunque which is incorporated in the document. And if the date of the MS. be, as we have shewn reason for supposing, not later than 680 or 670, then the date of the Quicunque itself must be carried back at latest to the middle or the earlier part of the same century; indeed, for anything that appears to the contrary, to a much earlier date [r].

[q] "His temporibus audiens Theodorus fidem Ecclesiæ Constantinopoli per hæresin Eutychetis multum esse turbatum, et Ecclesias Anglorum quibus præerat, ab hujusmodi labe immunes perdurare desiderans, collecto venerabilium sacerdotum doctorumque plurimorum cœtu, cujus essent fidei singuli sedulus inquirebat, omniumque unanimum in fide Catholica reperit consensum." *Hist. Eccles.* 4. c. 17.

[r] Waterland sees in the omission an indication that "the

This is the earliest date, so far as I am aware, that we can reach on external warranty. Waterland, ascribing the Commentary, *Junius* 25, to Venantius Fortunatus, would reach 570. And indeed, though we have no sufficient ground on which to rest Venantius's claim, there is nothing in the Commentary itself which would preclude that date or even an earlier.

ii. INTERNAL CONSIDERATIONS.

Internal considerations are often precarious. But yet there are certain characteristics in the Quicunque which, if they do not afford positive evidence as to its date, have at least a negative significance.

The Creed cannot have been composed before the rise of the Arian and Apollinarian controversies, for it has distinct reference to both of these heresies. It cannot have been written before the publication of some of St. Augustine's writings, especially of his book on the Trinity, for its language is plainly Augustinian. For a like reason, it cannot have been written before the publication of the Commonitory of Vincentius Lirinensis, unless indeed Vincentius himself was the author[s]. This makes its limit on the earlier side somewhere about 430. On the later side, as Waterland argues, it must have been written before the Eutychian and Nestorian controversies became rife, otherwise in the one case we should

---

Eutychian controversy was at its height," but would place that at the end of the fifth century or the beginning of the sixth. *Works*, vol. iii. p. 154.

[s] Vincentius's Commonitory was written in 434.

hardly have had the illustration, "As the reasonable soul and flesh is one man, so God and Man is one Christ," which, after the Eutychian times, the Catholics were shy of using, on account of the advantage taken of it by their opponents; and in the other we should have had language more distinctly and pointedly guarding against Nestorianism, especially the term Θεοτόκος, or rather its Latin equivalent, which, after the rise of Nestorianism, was rarely omitted in documents of this kind. These considerations seem to narrow the limit on the later side to the middle or the latter part of the fifth century. It is observable that the Creed bears no trace of either the Monothelete or the Adoptionist Controversy[t].

On the whole, however, I am not disposed to press the argument from internal considerations, though I am far from regarding it as of no account. I think it safest to rest upon the proof furnished by the external evidence which has been given above. For anything that appears to the contrary, the Creed may have been written at some time in the fifth century; but all that I venture to assert is that it was in existence in the middle or the earlier part of the seventh.

Even then it was of sufficient notoriety, and re-

[t] On the internal evidence see Waterland, who goes into the discussion at some length. Ch. 7. Dr. Pusey believed that " ts language fixes it as belonging to the 4th or 5th centuries." *On the Clause 'and the Son,'* p. 51. Its Augustinian phrases, however, are hardly consistent with the earlier of these dates, though some of them are found in the *De Fide et Symbolo*, the date of which is 393.

garded as important enough to be incorporated in a Sermon or Commentary, for such would seem to be the Treves Extract in the Colbert Manuscript. In the following century, if not earlier, to retrace our steps, we meet with it as the subject of an Exposition, of some length, (*Junius* 25), which again implies its previous existence, and that of sufficient duration for it to have acquired notoriety. At the close of that century we find it supplying the substance of a Bishop's Confession of Faith, put forth on his Consecration. Thus it would seem to have been gradually growing in estimation. Towards the end of the same century it begins to appear among the Hymns and Canticles at the end of Psalters, which would imply that it was coming into use in the Church's Offices.

These Psalters usually ascribe it, in the title prefixed, to St. Athanasius. And his name, together with the Service of which the Creed was found to be in the Processionist Controversy, speedily raised it to the important position which it has held in the Western Church for the last thousand years. In the East it has never been authoritatively sanctioned. The Orthodox Eastern Church recognizes but one Creed as of authority, the Constantinopolitan in its original, uninterpolated form. The Athanasian Creed, like the Apostles', is simply Western.

And to this, indeed, both its structure and the language in which it was originally written plainly point.

As to its structure it is neither more nor less than an enlargement of the Western Creed, the so-called "Apostles'," in Articles I., II., VIII., and III., the remaining Articles being added for the most part in the very words of the original.

As to the language—this, without question, was Latin, for though several Greek manuscripts are in existence, they are all of comparatively recent date, and, what is more to the point, they vary so much from one another, that they cannot possibly have been derived from one and the same Greek original. Their variations can be accounted for on no other supposition than that they are translations made by different hands: while, on the other hand, the Latin manuscripts have no other discrepancies than such as might be looked for in texts which have descended by repeated transcription from a common original.

As to the author—various conjectures have been hazarded. One thing at least is plain; it was not Athanasius. Athanasius died in 373, and the Creed cannot have been written so early. Waterland suggests Hilary, Bishop of Arles, one of the most eminent of the Gallican bishops who were living at the time at which he supposes the Creed to have been framed. Vincentius of Lerins, a contemporary of Hilary, has also been suggested [u], and, as it seems to me, with more reason. There are at least some very remarkable coincidences of language in his Commonitory with the Quicunque [x]. But where there is in truth so much uncertainty, even as to the date of the document, it is infinitely precarious to hazard a conjecture as to the author. We must be content to leave this, with many other questions of interest, unsolved.

[u] By Antelmi, *Nova de Symbolo Athanasiano Disquisitio.*
[x] See below, pp. 138, 139.

THE QUICUNQUE VULT, COMMONLY CALLED THE ATHANASIAN CREED.

1. Quicunque vult salvus esse, ante omnia opus est ut teneat Catholicam Fidem.

2. Quam nisi quisque integram inviolatamque servaverit, absque dubio in æternum peribit.

I., II., VIII.

3. Fides autem Catholica hæc est, ut unum Deum in Trinitate, et Trinitatem in Unitate veneremur:

4. Neque confundentes Personas, neque Substantiam separantes.

5. Alia est enim Persona Patris, alia Filii, alia Spiritus Sancti.

6. Sed Patris, et Filii et Spiritus Sancti, una est Divinitas, æqualis Gloria, coæterna Majestas.

7. Qualis Pater, talis Filius, talis et Spiritus Sanctus.

8. Increatus Pater, increatus Filius, increatus et Spiritus Sanctus.

9. Immensus Pater, immensus Filius, immensus et Spiritus Sanctus.

10. Æternus Pater, æternus Filius, æternus et Spiritus Sanctus.

11. Et tamen non tres æterni, sed unus æternus.

12. Sicut non tres increati, nec tres immensi, sed unus increatus, et unus immensus.

13. Similiter, Omnipotens Pater, Omnipotens Filius, Omnipotens et Spiritus Sanctus.

14. Et tamen non tres Omnipotentes, sed unus Omnipotens.

15. Ita Deus Pater, Deus Filius, Deus et Spiritus Sanctus.

16. Et tamen non tres Dii, sed unus est Deus.

17. Ita Dominus Pater, Dominus Filius, Dominus et Spiritus Sanctus.

18. Et tamen non tres Domini, sed unus est Dominus.

19. Quia sicut singillatim unamquamque Personam et Deum et Dominum confiteri Christiana veritate compellimur, ita tres Deos aut Dominos dicere Catholica religione prohibemur.

20. Pater a nullo est factus, nec creatus, nec genitus.

21. Filius a Patre solo est, non factus, nec creatus, sed genitus.

22. Spiritus Sanctus a Patre et Filio, non factus, nec creatus, nec genitus est, sed procedens.

23. Unus ergo Pater, non tres Patres; unus Filius, non tres Filii; unus Spiritus Sanctus, non tres Spiritus Sancti.

24. Et in hac Trinitate nihil prius aut posterius, nihil majus aut minus, sed totæ tres Personæ coæternæ sibi sunt, et coæquales.

25. Ita ut per omnia, sicut jam supra dictum est, et Unitas in Trinitate, et Trinitas in Unitate veneranda sit.

26. Qui vult ergo salvus esse, ita de Trinitate sentiat.

III.

27. Sed necessarium est ad æternam salutem, ut Incarnationem quoque Domini nostri Jesu Christi fideliter credat.

28. Est ergo Fides recta, ut credamus et confiteamur, quia Dominus noster Jesus Christus, Dei Filius, Deus pariter et Homo est.

29. Deus est ex substantia Patris ante sæcula genitus; Homo ex substantia Matris in sæculo natus.

30. Perfectus Deus, perfectus Homo, ex anima rationali et humana carne subsistens.

31. Æqualis Patri secundum Divinitatem; minor Patre secundum Humanitatem.

32. Qui licet Deus sit et Homo, non duo tamen, sed unus est Christus.

33. Unus autem, non conversione Divinitatis in carnem [a], sed adsumptione Humanitatis in Deum [y].

34. Unus omnino, non confusione Substantiæ, sed unitate Personæ.

35. Nam sicut anima rationalis et caro unus est Homo, ita Deus et Homo unus est Christus.

---

[y] There is very strong reason for believing that "in carne" and "in Deo" was the original text. Waterland prefers the commonly received reading, which, he says, has the support "of many MSS. of the Creed and of the Ambrosian MS. of Fortunatus's Commentary." And yet he acknowledges that the Colbert-Treves, the Ambrosian, the St. Germain's MSS. of the Creed, "aliique plurimi et vetusti," have "in carne" and "in Deo." He might have added the Utrecht MS. of the Creed and the Bodleian MS. of Fortunatus. The fact is that all the most ancient MSS. read "in carne" and "in Deo," which, by the way, is more likely to have been changed into "in carnem" and "in Deum" than the converse. Professor Swainson specifies thirty-three MSS., "including all the most ancient ones," which have "in carne" and "in Deo." *Nicene and Apostles' Creeds*, p. 532.

IV.—XII.

36. Qui passus est pro salute nostra;
37. Descendit ad inferos[1];
   Tertia die resurrexit a mortuis;
38. Adscendit ad cœlos;
   Sedet ad dexteram Patris;
39. Inde venturus judicare vivos et mortuos.
40. Ad cujus adventum omnes homines resurgere habent cum corporibus suis, et reddituri sunt de factis propriis rationem;
41. Et qui bona egerunt, ibunt in vitam æternam; qui vero mala, in ignem æternum;
42. Hæc est Fides Catholica, quam nisi quisque fideliter firmiterque crediderit salvus esse non poterit.

---

[1] Ad inferos. The Bodl. MS. of Fortunatus's Commentary reads "ad inferna." On which Waterland remarks (p. 267) "Q. anon vetustissima hæc fuerit lectio in Symbolo Athanasiano, sicut in Apostolico?" It is the reading of the Colbert-Treves, the Utrecht, and the St. Germain's MSS. When in the Apostles' Creed *inferos* was substituted for *inferna*, the Athanasian, it would seem, was altered conformably. It is worth noticing that "Sedet ad dexteram Patris" of v. 38, which was the earlier form of the Apostles' Creed, remained unaltered in the Athanasian. If the Athanasian Creed had been framed at the time when "sedet at dexteram *Dei* Patris *Omnipotentis*" was the established reading of the Apostles' Creed, such also, in all probability, would have been the text of the Athanasian. These are worth notice as among the minuter indications of the early age of the Creed.

APPENDIX I.

THE QUICUNQUE AND THE TREVES MS. COMPARED.

QUICUNQUE.	TREVES MS.
Sed necessarium est ad æternam salutem ut Incarnationem quoque Domini nostri Jesu Christi fideliter credat.	. . . . Domini nostri Jesu Christi fideliter credat.
Est ergo fides recta ut credamus et confiteamur quia Dominus noster Jesus Christus, Dei Filius, Deus pariter et Homo est.	Est ergo fides recta ut credamus et confitemur quia Dominus . . . Jesus Christus Dei Filius Deus pariter et Homo est.
Deus est ex substantia Patris ante sæcula genitus, Homo ex substantia Matris in sæculo natus.	Deus est de substantia Patris ante sæcula genitus, et Homo de substantia Matris in sæculo natus.
Perfectus Deus, perfectus Homo ex anima rationali et humana carne subsistens.	Perfectus Deus, Perfectus Homo ex anima rationabili et humana carne subsistens.
Æqualis Patri secundum Divinitatem, minor Patre secundum Humanitatem.	Æqualis Patri secundum Divinitatem, minor Patri secundum Humanitatem.
Qui licet Deus sit et Homo, non duo tamen sed unus est Christus.	Qui licet Deus sit Homo, non duo tamen sed unus est Christus.

| QUICUNQUE. | TREVES MS. |

Unus autem non conversione Divinitatis in carnem [a], sed adsumptione Humanitatis in Deum [a].

Unus omnino non confusione substantiæ sed unitate Personæ.

Nam sicut anima rationalis et caro unus est homo, ita Deus et Homo unus est Christus.

Qui passus est pro salute nostra;

Descendit ad inferos [a];

Tertia die resurrexit a mortuis;

Ascendit ad cœlos,

Sedet ad dexteram Patris;

Inde venturus judicare vivos et mortuos.

Ad cujus adventum omnes homines resurgere habent cum corporibus suis,

Unus autem non ex eo quod sit in Carne [a] conversa Divinitas, sed quia est in Deo [a] adsumpta dignanter Humanitas.

Unus Christus est non confusione substantiæ sed unitatem Personæ.

. . . . . .
. . . . . .
. . . . . .

Qui secundum fidem nostram passus et mortuus;

Ad inferna [a] discendens;

Et die tertia resurrexit;

Atque ad cœlos ascendit,

Ad dexteram Dei Patris sedet,

Sicut vobis in Simbulo tradutum est;

Inde ad judicandos vivos et mortuos credimus et speramus Eum esse venturum.

Ad cujus adventum erunt omnes homines sine dubio in suis corporibus resurrecturi,

---

[a] It should be observed, as I have said in the preceding notes, that "in Carne" and "in Deo" and "ad inferna" are in all probability the original readings of the Quicunque. These being the readings also of the Treves MS., they afford an additional indication of the antiquity of that MS.

QUICUNQUE.	TREVES MS.
et reddituri sunt de factis propriis rationem.	et reddituri de factis propriis rationem.
Et qui bona egerunt ibunt in vitam æternam, qui vero mala in ignem æternum.	Ut qui bona egerunt eant in vitam æternam qui mala in ignem æternum.
Hæc est fides Catholica, quam nisi quisque fideliter firmiterque crediderit, salvus esse non poterit.	Hæc est fides sancta et Catholica quam omnis homo qui ad vitam æternam pervenire desiderat scire integre debet et fideliter custodire.

APPENDIX II.

The following Parallelisms between the language of the Quicunque and the Commonitory of Vincentius of Lerins are from Antelmi's *Nova de Symbolo Athanasiano Disquisitio* (Parisiis, 1693).

EXCERPTUM E SYMBOLO.

1. Fides autem Catholica hæc est ut unum Deum in Trinitate, et Trinitatem in Unitate veneremur.

2. Neque confundentes Personas, neque Substantiam separantes.

3. Alia est enim Persona Patris, alia Filii, alia Spiritus Sancti.

4. Sed Patris et Filii et Spiritus Sancti una est Divinitas, æqualis gloria, cœterna Majestas.

5. Est ergo fides recta ut credamus et confiteamur quia Dominus noster Jesus Christus, Dei Filius, Deus pariter et Homo est.

EXCERPTUM E COMMONITORIO.

1. Ecclesia vera Catholica unam Divinitatem in Trinitatis plenitudine, et Trinitatis æqualitatem in una atque eadem majestate veneratur.

2. Ut neque singularitas substantiæ personarum confundat proprietatem, neque item Trinitatis distinctio Unitatem separet Deitatis.

3. Quia scilicet alia est Persona Patris, alia Filii, alia Spiritus Sancti.

4. Sed Patris et Filii et Spiritus Sancti non alia et alia, sed una eademque natura.

5 . . . ut confiteamur . . unus idemque Christus Filius Dei, unus idem Christus Deus et Homo.

EXCERPTUM E SYMBOLO.

6. Deus est ex substantia Patris ante sæcula genitus; Homo ex substantia Matris, in sæculo natus.

7. Perfectus Deus, perfectus Homo; ex anima rationali et humana carne subsistens.

8. Æqualis Patri secundum Divinitatem; minor Patre secundum Humanitatem.

9. Qui licet Deus sit et Homo, non duo tamen, sed unus est Christus.

10. Unus autem non conversione Divinitatis in carnem, sed adsumptione Humanitatis in Deum.

11. Nam sicut anima rationalis et caro unus est Homo, ita Deus et Homo unus est Christus.

EXCERPTUM E COMMONITORIO.

6. Idem ex Patre ante sæcula genitus; idem ex Matre in Sæculo generatus.

7. Perfectus Deus, perfectus Homo; in Deo summa Divinitas, in homine plena humanitas, quippe quæ animam simul habeat et carnem.

8. Duæ substantiæ sunt, una coeterna, et æqualis Patri, altera ex tempore et minor Patre.

9. Unum Christum Jesum, non duos; Eundumque Deum pariter atque Hominem... et hoc totum unus est Christus.

10. Unus autem non.. Divinitatis et Humanitatis confusione, sed unitate Personæ.

11. Igitur sicut anima connexa carni non imitatur Hominem, sed est Homo, ita etiam Verbum Deus, uniendo se Homini.. factus est Homo, ... et ex duabus substantiis unus est Christus [a].

These passages will be found in Chapters XIII.—XVI. of the Commonitory.

CHAPTER V.

AN EXPOSITION OF THE QUICUNQUE VULT, COMMONLY CALLED THE ATHANASIAN CREED

"AFTER all, the only question of real importance is that which concerns the subject-matter of the Creed. If the Creed be in accordance with the Word of God, so that 'it may be proved by most certain warrants of Holy Scripture,' if it states the truth with precision and accuracy, so as to guard it against errors,—grave errors—not which may be imagined as of possible occurrence, but which have actually made havoc of the Church in time past, and may do so again, then it signifies little when or by whom it was put together. Its value is no whit diminished by the circumstance that its origin is concealed in the mist of antiquity, or that its author, like the authors of many others of our blessings, is to be numbered among our unknown benefactors."

CHAPTER V.

AN EXPOSITITION OF THE QUICUNQUE VULT, COMMONLY CALLED THE ATHANASIAN CREED.

THE "Quicunque," though popularly called a Creed, is not such technically,—not in the sense in which the Apostles' and Nicene Creeds are. Rather it is a brief Exposition of the Apostles' Creed in those Articles, I., II., VIII., which relate to the doctrine of the Trinity, and in Art. III. which relates to the doctrine of the Incarnation, with the special object of guarding them from the perversions of heresy, the remaining articles being added nearly word for word as they stand in the Apostles' Creed. No better account could be given both of its character and of its object than that which St. Augustine gives of his own Treatise on the Creed, de Fide et Symbolo[a]: "The exposition of the Faith serves for the defence of the Creed: its object being, not to provide a formulary to be learnt by heart and afterwards rehearsed by those who are seeking the grace of God in baptism, but to guard the truths contained in the Creed against the insidious devices of heretics with Catholic authority and a more secure defence."

This, which is the true view to be taken of the document, is important as qualifying the so-called damnatory clauses, and precluding the objection

De Fide et Symbolo, § 1.

founded upon the supposition that they apply to every minute detail. If the Quicunque be simply an Exposition of the Catholic Faith, then those damnatory clauses apply directly only to the Catholic Faith therein expounded. Indirectly it is true they do to the Exposition, so far as any of its statements involve the Catholic Faith itself, so far as the denial of any of them involves the denial of the Catholic Faith. But all do not, and even those which do are not to be put on a level with the great fundamental verities themselves. For it is not every one who doubts the soundness of one of these details who sees that the denial of it eventually overthrows one or another of the great fundamental verities.

That we may the better enter into the statements which we shall meet with, it will be well to prepare the way by a brief account of the heresies against which it is the object of the Creed to guard. These are:

I. On the doctrine of the Trinity, chiefly the Sabellian, the Arian, the Macedonian heresies.

II. On the doctrine of the Incarnation, the heresies of the Docetæ, the Arians, the Apollinarians, and, unless their rise was subsequent to the composition of the Creed, those of the Nestorians and Eutychians.

I. 1. The Sabellians "confounded the Persons." They were so intent on maintaining the unity of the Godhead, that they overlooked that distinction of Persons which Scripture everywhere intimates. The heresy in an earlier stage was called "Patripassian," from the circumstance that, looking upon the three

Divine Persons as one Person, it held the Father to have become incarnate, and to have suffered.

2. The Arians, on the other hand, "divided the substance." They not only recognized three several and distinct Persons, but they believed these to be of diverse natures,—the Father, God in the highest sense, the Son, God in an inferior sense, a creature though superior to all other creatures, and the Holy Spirit also a creature, created by the Son, and inferior to the Son.

3. The Macedonians were an offshoot from the Arians. They had abandoned the capital error of Arianism which they once held, the denial of the proper Deity of the Son, but they retained and set forth more explicitly and gave greater prominence to the other error just mentioned, the denial of the proper Deity of the Holy Ghost. They held that He is a ministering spirit, such as the Holy Angels are [b]. These also then "divided the substance."

II. With regard to the Incarnation:

1. The Docetæ denied the verity of our Lord's human nature. They held that the body in which He appeared was only a phantom body, an illusion. He did not really partake of flesh and blood, He did not really suffer, He did not really die.

2. The Arians erred not only as to our Lord's Deity, but as to His manhood also. In their view He was not "perfect man." For whereas man consists of body and soul, while they held that our Lord had a true human body, they denied that He had a human

[b] Sozom. 4. 27. It should be noted that both Arians and Macedonians acknowledged the Personality of the Holy Spirit.

soul. The Λόγος, the Divine Word, supplied its place.

3. And in this the Apollinarians, though they were orthodox as to our Lord's Deity, agreed with them, only they differed on a point of philosophy. For while the Arians divided man into two parts, body and soul, the Apollinarians divided him into three, body, animal soul (anima, ψυχή), and rational soul (animus, πνεῦμα, νοῦς [c]). The two former they held that our Lord had in common with men in general; the place of the last-mentioned, the rational soul, they believed to be supplied by the divine Word.

It was to guard, then, against the errors of both the Arians and the Apollinarians, as well as against those of the Docetæ, that those words were inserted, "perfect man," "of a reasonable soul and human flesh subsisting."

The Apollinarians further denied that the body which our Lord had was derived from His Mother. He brought it down from heaven, they said, misinterpreting such texts as St. John iii. 13, "No man hath ascended up to heaven, but He that came down from heaven." They denied then that He was "man of the substance of his mother."

But further, they held a doctrine, naturally enough growing out of their persuasion that the Λόγος supplied in Christ the place of the rational soul, and near akin to that which was afterwards called Eutychianism, the confusion of the two natures; and they often charged the Catholics with holding what was afterwards called Nestorianism, the separating of Christ into two Persons. This, as Waterland ob-

[c] See 1 Thess. v. 23.

serves, "led the Catholics, in their condemnation of the Apollinarians, to condemn the Eutychian doctrine before Eutyches, and in their defence of themselves to condemn the Nestorian doctrine before Nestorius." It was in reference to this tenet that the Eutychians were often charged with reviving Apollinarianism [d].

It is possible, then, that the author of the Quicunque had neither Eutychianism nor Nestorianism in view, and that the passages which would appear to be pointedly aimed against those heresies, though they undesignedly anticipated them, were framed without reference to them. It is remarkable that the Exposition of the Creed ascribed to Fortunatus [e], though it refers to Apollinaris by name, makes no mention either of Nestorianism or Eutychianism, or indeed of any heresy whose rise was subsequent to that of Apollinarianism.

However, to speak briefly of each of those heresies:

4. The Nestorians "divided Christ into two Persons—the Son of God and the Son of Man: the one a Person begotten of God before all worlds, the other also a Person, born of the Virgin Mary, and in special favour chosen to be made entire to the Son of God, so that whosoever will honour God must together honour Christ, with whose Person God hath vouchsafed to join Himself [f]."

5. Eutychianism was a recoil from Nestorianism. The Eutychians, in their dread of the sundering of Christ into two Persons, confounded the natures.

---
[d] Waterland, vol. iii. p. 206, Oxford, 1843.
[e] *Junius* 25, see above, p. 322.   [f] Hooker, E. P., v. 53, § 2.

They held that the human nature was so wholly swallowed up in the divine that from the moment of the union it ceased to be.

Verses 32-35 of the Quicunque might seem to have been aimed at these heresies; but, as has just been observed, their language may be sufficiently accounted for even if they were written before those heresies had become prominent. And indeed verse 33, "One not by conversion of the Godhead into flesh, but by taking of the manhood into God," though pointedly opposed to one form at least of the Apollinarian teaching does not touch the Eutychian. The Eutychians held the converse, the absorption of the human nature by the divine. It should be added, that, as Waterland remarks, other characteristics are wanting which could hardly have been absent if the Quicunque had been written while Nestorianism or Eutychianism were prevalent.

To proceed now with the Exposition: The Creed, or let me rather say, the Exposition, begins by declaring the importance of holding, and holding fast to the end, the Catholic Faith. "Whosoever" would be saved (vult salvus esse), before all things it is necessary that he hold the Catholic Faith, which faith except every one shall have kept (servaverit), shall have kept to the end f, whole and undefiled, without doubt he shall perish eternally (in æternum peribit).

These are awful words, and as such they have been a source of distress and perplexity to some, an occasion of cavil and vituperation to others.

But in truth they are but an echo of our Lord's

f See 2 Tim. iv. 7.

warning, "He that believeth and is baptized shall be saved; but he that believeth not shall be damned [g];" "He that believeth on the Son hath everlasting life; and he that believeth not the Son shall not see life, but the wrath of God abideth on him [h]."

"Do we think," as the case has been well put, "that the expression of our Lord, general and unlimited as it is, does yet admit of all merciful allowance for non-belief arising from invincible or excusable ignorance, for misbelief arising from mere error, from prejudice, from education, from unhappy circumstances of any kind? So also we understand the Creed. It applies the same solemn sanction of our Lord to the truths which He commissioned His apostles to teach, and leaves it unlimited as He left it. The presumption would have been, not in adopting His language, but in qualifying what He has not authorised man to qualify; the want of charity, not in announcing the danger to which infidelity is exposed, but in dissembling or extenuating it. If the Creed is not expressed as it might and probably would be expressed, if it were drawn up anew, it is sufficient to say, that the advantage of adhering to an old and recognised formulary more than counterbalances any prospect of amended diction [i]."

It might be urged perhaps that our Lord's words above quoted refer simply to the general belief in Himself as the Messiah, not to this or the other par-

---

[h] Mark xvi. 16.   [i] John iii. 36.
[j] Bp. Phillpott's Letter to Earl Grey, June 30, 1819, republished by the Bishop together with his Letters to Charles Butler in 1866.

ticular in the detail of Christian doctrine. But it will be remembered that His Apostles use language equally strong of particular truths. We need only refer, for instance, to St. Paul's words directed against those who were corrupting the doctrine of Justification by faith, Gal. i. 6-9, and against those who were denying the truth of the Resurrection, 2 Tim. ii. 17, 18, and 1 Tim. i. 19, 20, or to St. John's warnings in reference to those who were denying the verity of our Lord's human nature, 1 John iv. 2, 3, 2 John 6, 11, warnings the more to be noted, as exhibited by that Apostle who was eminently the Apostle of love, warnings which, however the world might regard them, were themselves the utterances of love, of love which arrays itself with the instinct of parental affection against those who would injure the objects of its regard.

It is true that many of the statements of the Athanasian Creed are abstruse, and beyond the comprehension of persons who have not made the subjects to which they relate their study. But it is to be borne in mind that such also are the heterodox statements to guard against which they were introduced. They would not have been ventured upon if heresy had not constrained the Church to define what otherwise she would have preferred to leave undefined. "Every one of them," that I may adopt the language of an eminent living divine in reference to another Formulary, "if it is not so now, was once the negation of some existing error—not a mere imagination of what it might be necessary to counteract, but founded upon an actual experience of that necessity—

a protest against something which might be advanced on the side of heterodoxy, even because it had already been so advanced, and had wrought some serious breach in the unity and in the completeness of the faith once delivered to the saints[k]."

These considerations are sufficient not only to justify, but to enhance the value of those abstruse statements with which the Creed deals, while, at the same time, they account for the strong language with which it guards them.

I. The Creed, after stating summarily, in verses 3 and 4, what the Catholic Faith is, as regards one great fundamental truth, which it behoves every one to hold, proceeds in the verses which follow (5-25) to enlarge upon that truth, on the one hand for its more distinct enunciation, on the other, for the guarding of it from misapprehension or perversion.

"The Catholic Faith is this, that we worship one God in Trinity and Trinity in Unity: neither confounding the Persons, nor dividing the Substance."

I will not enter into the discussion which has been raised as to the propriety of the terms "Substance" and "Person." No terms which human thought can devise can adequately express the things which they represent: but these have a conventional meaning which is sufficiently understood; and that meaning rests on a solid Scriptural foundation.

On the one hand, no truth stands out with greater

---

[k] The present Dean of Llandaff, Dr. Vaughan, in reference to the XXXIX Articles. "Against which poison if we think that the Church of this day needeth not those ancient preservatives which ages before us were so glad to use, we deceive ourselves greatly." *Hooker, E. P.*, v. 43.

prominence throughout the sacred volume, than that God is one, and but one; on the other, not only is the Father called God, but the Son likewise; and the Holy Spirit is joined with both in that solemn formula which declares the Name of that God to whom the Christian at his baptism is consecrated. Under the Patriarchal dispensation God revealed Himself by the name of GOD ALMIGHTY, under the Mosaic by the name of JEHOVAH (Exod. vi. 3); when the Christian Dispensation was founded God revealed Himself by a new name: the Converts were to be baptized, not into the name of GOD ALMIGHTY, not into the name of JEHOVAH, but into the name of THE FATHER AND OF THE SON AND OF THE HOLY GHOST. We believe therefore that the Father is God, that the Son is God, and that the Holy Ghost is God, and we speak of each, when we speak of them separately, for want of a more adequate word, as a Person; and yet bearing in mind the jealous care with which Scripture guards the doctrine of the Unity of the Godhead, we do not venture to think of them as other than one God, which we should do if we were to divide or separate the substance, that is, if we were to regard the nature of one of these divine Persons as diverse from that of another.

"For," so the Creed proceeds, enlarging upon the statements already made, "There is one Person of the Father, another of the Son, and another of the Holy Ghost." To deny this, as the Sabellians did, would be to "confound the Persons," in direct contradiction to the teaching of Scripture which uniformly distinguishes them [1].

---

[1] See e.g. Mat. iii. 16; Ephes. ii. 18; Gal. iv. 4-6.

" But the Godhead of the Father, of the Son, and of the Holy Ghost is all one, the glory equal, the majesty co-eternal." To deny this, as the Arians and Macedonians did, would be to divide or separate the Substance, to imply that there are more Gods than one, which also directly contradicts the express teaching of Scripture [m].

The verses which follow, to the 19th inclusive, are simply an expansion of the truth contained in the preceding verse. To hold, e.g., as the Arians did, that the Son and the Holy Spirit are not such, as to their nature or their attributes, as the Father, that while the Father is uncreate, is incomprehensible (infinite), is eternal, is almighty, the Son and the Holy Spirit are created beings, however high in the scale of creation, that they are comprehensible (finite), that they are not eternal, not almighty, would be to strip them of the necessary and inseparable attributes of Godhead, to represent them as God only in an improper, secondary, inferior sense, and consequently, if the name of God be in any case given them, to make three Gods, not one God.

On the other hand, while we assign to each of these divine Persons all the attributes of Godhead, we must be circumspect in our language, lest we should infringe the doctrine of the divine unity in another way. We must not speak of three eternal Beings, three uncreated Beings, three incomprehensible or infinite Beings, three Almighty Beings. This also would be in effect to represent them as three Gods, not one God.

[m] Deut. vi. 4; Mat. xxviii. 19.

Language of the description just referred to is frequent with St. Augustine, though rarely used before his time. "The Greeks never used it, but taught the same thing under a different form of expression. What Greeks and Latins both intended was, that as the three Persons are one Substance and one God, so every divine perfection, and every substantial attribute belonging to any one Person is common to all, and there is nothing peculiar to any one but the divine relations—to the Father Paternity and whatever it implies or carries with it, to the Son Filiation, to the Holy Ghost Procession[a]."

Thus then, to recapitulate what has been said, for this is the sum and substance of it—"The Father is God, the Son is God, and the Holy Ghost is God; and yet there are not three Gods but one God. In like manner, the Father is Lord, the Son is Lord, and the Holy Ghost is Lord; and yet there are not three Lords but one Lord. For like as we are compelled by the Christian verity to acknowledge each person severally to be God and Lord, so are we forbidden by the Catholic religion to say there be three Gods or three Lords."

So much for guarding against "separating the Substance." Now to guard in like manner against "confounding the Persons."

Each of the divine Persons has his own distinctive property or characteristic, and as He has it so we must be careful to preserve it.

The property of the Father is to be "of none." His being is derived from none. He is "not made," He is "not created," He is "not begotten.".

[a] Waterland, Vol. 3, p. 233.

The property of the Son is to be "of the Father," and, in view of what is said in reference to the Holy Spirit in the next verse, "of the Father alone;" yet not "made," "not created," but "begotten."

The property of the Holy Ghost is to be "of the Father and the Son," yet "not made," "not created," "not begotten," "but proceeding."

Yet when we speak of the Holy Ghost as proceeding from the Father and the Son, we must not think of two co-ordinate sources of His being. There is but one original fountain of existence. To speak of two would be to acknowledge two Gods, which is the charge which the Greeks bring against the Western Church, though altogether unwarrantably, grounded upon this doctrine of the double procession. Yet the whole subject is involved in mystery. Whatever we venture to say respecting it, we must say with unfeigned diffidence and humility, not venturing a step beyond the limits which Scripture has marked out for us. Pity that on such a subject so much exasperation of feeling should have been stirred up. No one surely at the present day who accepts the Quicunque would think of so interpreting its language as to imply that to hold the Greek doctrine of the single procession is incompatible with a state of salvation. That doctrine does not either directly or by consequence overthrow the doctrine of the Trinity. The Eastern and Western Churches on this point are really at one, only they cannot agree to adopt one and the same formula.

Having thus indicated the characteristics by which the divine Persons are severally distinguished, the

Creed winds up what is to be said on this point. "So there is one Father, not three Fathers, one Son, not three Sons, one Holy Ghost, not three Holy Ghosts."

"And in this Trinity none is afore or after other, none is greater or less than another"—there is no such thing as afore or after, there is no such thing as greater or less—to affirm this would again be to divide or separate the substance, in fact to teach a plurality of Gods: "but all the three Persons are co-eternal together," as opposed to afore or after, "and co-equal," as opposed to greater or less.

"So that in all things, as is aforesaid," viz. in v. 3, "the Unity in Trinity and the Trinity in Unity is to be worshipped. We are in such wise to worship the one God as to acknowledge a Trinity of Persons; in such wise to acknowledge a Trinity of Persons as yet to worship but one God.

"He therefore who would be saved must thus think of the Trinity."

Here we close the first great division of the Creed. It has one and but one subject, the doctrine of the Trinity in Unity, the doctrine that there is one God and but one, and yet that in the Unity of the Godhead there are three divine Persons. All the several details which occupy vv. 5-24 inclusive are simply designed to guard this doctrine, and whatever importance attaches to them attaches to them simply as they are related to it, and the warning clauses so far as they apply to them apply to them only in that respect. If any of them are not essential to the guarding of that doctrine, to such the warning clauses are not to be extended, and it is on this ground that the question of the Procession of the Holy Spirit from the Son as well as from the Father may well be looked upon as beyond their range.

II. We now come to the second of those great verities which it is the special object of the Creed to guard from perversion—the Incarnation of the Son of God.

"Furthermore, It is necessary to eternal salvation that we also believe rightly the Incarnation of our Lord Jesus Christ."

"For the right faith is, that we believe and confess, that our Lord Jesus Christ, the Son of God, is God and Man, as well the one as the other:" God, as the Son of God, Man, as born of a woman. "God of the substance of the Father," of the same nature as the Father (as a human son is of the same nature with his human father), "begotten before the worlds (ante secula genitus)," before time began; "Man, of the substance of his mother," human as she was human, "born in the world (in sæculo natus)," born in time.

That He is God, God in the highest sense, "perfect God," is set forth in Scripture in many ways, direct and indirect; that He is man, "man of the substance of his mother," this also is distinctly taught, as e.g. where He is spoken of as "the fruit of her womb:" and that He is "perfect man," man in the strictest sense, man in all respects as we are, sin only except, "of a reasonable, rational soul and human flesh subsisting," this also is plain from the whole history of His life. Plain, however, as it is, it is the more necessary to affirm it in express words, because there were heretics who denied that our Lord had a human body, and others who denied that He had a human soul.

"Equal to the Father, as touching His Godhead." This He must needs be if He be very God; "inferior to the Father, as touching His manhood," which requires no proof.

"Who, though He be God and Man, yet He is not two"—two Persons—as the Catholics were sometimes falsely charged with teaching, and as the Nestorians did actually teach, "but one Christ." For while we read in plain terms of two distinct natures, we have no warrant for believing two Persons. That Divine Word, which "was in the beginning with God," and "was God," is the same Person who in the fulness of time "was made flesh and dwelt among us°."

"One, however, not by conversion of the Godhead into flesh," of the divine nature into the human, as the Apollinarians sometimes taught, (for how could the infinite and immutable Godhead be capable of conversion or change?) "but by taking of the manhood into God," by associating the human nature with the divine, in His one Person. Μένων ὃ ἦν ἔλαβεν ὃ οὐκ ἦν, Remaining what He was He took what He was not.

"One altogether—one and but one—not by confusion of substance, but by unity of Person." One, that is, not by blending the human nature with the Divine, which would have been to produce a mixed nature, neither human nor divine, a hypothesis not

° St. John i. 1 and 14.

only derogatory to the divine nature, but contrary to the express teaching of Scripture in such passages as 1 Tim. ii. 5. "There is one Mediator between God and Man, Himself Man, Christ Jesus." "One," then, "not by confusion of substance," as the Apollinarians first, and the Eutychians afterwards taught, "but by oneness of Person."

"For," if we may venture, in so high a matter, to use an illustration drawn from earthly things, "as the reasonable, the rational, soul and flesh, the soul and body, is one man, so God and Man is one Christ."

This closes that part of the Quicunque which relates to the Incarnation, so far as the doctrine is contained in the third Article of the Apostles' Creed [p]. If it ventures upon matters, some of which may well seem too high for human reach, it should be remembered, as was said above, that it has done so by constraint. If heresy had not perverted the truth, the Church would have been well content to use the simpler language of her earlier Formularies. But when erroneous statements were put forward and were gaining acceptance, it became necessary to meet them. As it has been well said, to use the words of one of the early Fathers, "It is the fault of heretics that we are forced to do things which ought not to be done, to climb heights on which no human foot ought to tread, to speak words which ought not to be spoken, to venture upon subjects which it is

[p] In strictness the following Articles also, IV., V., VI., VII., relate to the same doctrine, but the Quicunque does little more than repeat them, as they stand in the Apostles' Creed.

not permitted to handle, and when it behoves us to fulfil what is enjoined by faith and by faith alone,— to adore, that is, the Father, together with Him to worship the Son, and to abound in the Holy Ghost, we are forced to stretch our feeble speech to things which are beyond the reach of speech, and by other men's fault are constrained to be guilty of a fault ourselves q."

The remainder of the Quicunque needs no special comment. It repeats Articles IV., V., VI., VII., nearly in the words of the Apostles' Creed, as we now have it. It omits Arts. IX. and X., no controversy being occurrent with regard to the subjects of those Articles. On Arts. XI. and XII. it is somewhat fuller, and more precise: "At whose coming all men shall rise again with their bodies, and shall give account for their own works: and they that have done good shall go into life eternal, and they that have done evil into eternal fire." The error said to have been first broached by Origen, and afterwards held by those who from him were called Origenists, was probably glanced at. It was to the effect that wicked men, and even the Evil One himself, will, in the revolution of ages, be released from punishment. In opposition to this the Creed declares expressly, and almost in the very words of Scripture, that the sufferings of the ungodly, equally with the joys of the righteous, will have no end. The same measure, eternity, which defines the duration of the one, defines also, as it does in Scripture, the dura-

q Hilar. *de Trinitate*, ii. § 2.

tion of the other. You cannot lighten the sinner's dread without in the same proportion paring away from the saint's hope.

The last verse gathers up the whole, and the Creed closes as it began, "This is the Catholic faith, which except a man believe faithfully he cannot be saved."

I need only glance at what I have already said of these solemn warnings. It must be confessed that they have a harsh sound to modern ears. But this is (1) partly because it is not understood to what they apply, (2) partly because it is not considered with what limitations they are to be taken, (3) partly because it is not borne in mind in what terms Scripture speaks of misbelief and unbelief.

(1) The aim of the Creed, as has been said, is to throw its shield principally around two great doctrines, the Trinity in Unity and the Incarnation. No rightly instructed Christian will deny that the belief of these, as of the other cardinal verities of Christianity, is necessary to salvation; and all that the damnatory or warning clauses amount to is to assert the indispensable necessity of such belief.

(2) These clauses must always be understood with such qualifications and limitations as the reason of things suggests. It is not to be supposed that the peril of which they speak is incurred by every one who does not explicitly hold every particular statement which the Creed contains, though undoubtedly it is by those who, having had full opportunity of learning the truth, obstinately and persistently deny either the great fundamental verities with which it is concerned, or any of the particulars

which by necessary consequence involve any of those verities.

(3) What will be the case of those who have erred in these matters through ignorance over which they have had no control, whose unbelief or misbelief has been inherited, for instance, we know not, neither does the Creed pronounce. Only certainly there is enough shewn us, even in God's natural dealing with the world, to make us watchful over ourselves and circumspect as regards others. Even ignorance or oversight may have consequences in spiritual matters, as they undoubtedly often have in temporal, of the gravest description.

INDEX.

Adoptionist Controversy, 128
Alcuin, 32
Alexander, Bp. of Alexandria, 51
Ambrose, St., 55, 62
Ambrosian MS. of Athanasian Creed, 124
Anastasius, 105
Anathema, Nicene, 59, 65
Anathema appended to Epiphanius's Creed, 82
Anathemas appended to Cyril's 3rd Epistle, 105
Antelmi, 130, 138
Apollinaris, 84
Apollinarian Heresy, 146, 158
Apostolic Constitutions, 70
Apostolic Constitutions, Coptic, 96
Apostolic Origin of the Creed, 3, 5
Apostolicum Symbolum not peculiar as a Title to the Western Creed, 8
Arian Heresy, 145, 153
Arius, 51, 85
Athanasius, St., 54, 68, 130
Augustine, St., 18, 144

Baptism. Interrogatories at, 23, 37, 95
—— Renunciations at, 49, 73, 96
—— Times of Celebration, 12
Bede, 126

Biclaro, John, Abbot of, 89
Bull, Bp., 5, 34, 65, 87
Bryennius, 71

Catechumens, Instruction of, 72
Chalcedon Definition of Faith, 103, 109
Charlemagne, 16, 120
Colbert MS., 124
"Communion of Saints," date of insertion, 35
Constantine, 54, 67
Constantius, 57, 67
Cotton, Sir Robert, 115, 118
Councils—Nicæa (A.D. 325), 54
—— Constantinople (A.D. 381), 82
—— Ephesus (A.D. 431), 112
—— Ephesus (Latrocinium, A.D. 449), 107
—— Chalcedon (A.D. 451), 105
—— Toledo, 3rd (A.D. 589), 88
—— Hethfeld (A.D. 680), 126
—— Trullan (A.D. 692), 71
Creed—its origin, 6
—— concealed from the uninitiated, 7
—— earliest Liturgical use, 9, 11
Creeds, Western—Declarative, 19 sqq.
—— Irenæus, St., 20

Creeds, Tertullian, 22
— Cyprian, St., 23
— Carthage, 24
— Marcellus, 25
— Aquileia (Rufinus), 27
— Roman, 4th and 5th centuries, 29
— Present form, 31
Creeds, Western—Interrogative, 37 sqq.
— Cyprian, St., 37
— Milan (St. Ambrose), 38
— Rome (Gelasian Sacramentary), 38
— Salisbury Manual, 39
— Book of Common Prayer, 39
Creeds, Eastern—Declarative, 49 sqq.
— Jerusalem, 50, 75
— Cæsarea (Eusebius), 57
— Nicæa, 58
— Alexandria, 66
— Arius and Euzoius, 68
— Apostolic Constitutions, 73
— Epiphanius, 78, 79
— Constantinople, 82, 93
— Coptic Constitutions, 97
Creeds, Eastern—Interrogative, 95 sqq.
— Jerusalem, 95
— Apostolic Constitutions, 73
— Coptic, 97
Creeds, Apostles' and Nicene Harmonised, 42
Creed of St. Athanasius, History of, 115
— Exposition of, 143
— MSS. of, 119, 120, 124, 129, 135
— Heresies guarded against, 144
— Warning Clauses, 143, 156, 161
Cyril, St., of Alexandria—his Epistles, 105, 108, 112

Cyril, St., of Jerusalem, 49, 75
Χριστοτόκος, 104

Dates of added clauses in Western Creed, 32
Denebert, 121
Descendit ad inferna, 28, 33
Dioscorus, 107
Docetæ, 145
Διδαχὴ τῶν δώδεκα ἀποστόλων, 71

Ephesus 7th Canon of Council, 114
Epiphanius, 71, 76
Erasmus censured for denying the Apostolic origin of the Creed, 3
Euphemia, St., Martyr Chapel of, 108
Eusebius of Cæsarea, 56
— Remarks on his Creed, 60
Eusebius, of Nicomedia, 56
Eustathius, 56
Eutyches, 106
Eutychianism, 147
Euzoius, 67
Ἔκθεσις, 8, 110

Ffoulkes, Mr., 11, 116
Filioque, 88, 94, 155
Flavian, 106

Hell, Descent into, 28, 33
Hethfeld, Synod of, 91, 126
Hilary of Arles, 116, 130
Hilary of Poictiers, 106, 159
Hooker, 48
Hosius, 54, 57

Jerome, St., 60
Jerusalem—supposed the centre of the earth, 21
Jerusalem, Latin Monks of, 121
Incarnation, Doctrine of, 111; 157
Irenæus, St., 19
Julius, Bp. of Rome, 25
Junius (25), 122

INDEX.

Kaye, Bp., Council of Nicæa, 60, 64
King, Lord, Critical History of the Creed, 5, 7

Latrocinium, 107
Leo, St., 29, 107, 108
────── his Epistle to Flavian, 113
Leo III. refuses to sanction the insertion of the Filioque, 90
────── The Tables of, 91
Lumby, Dr., 117, 120
Δαμβανόμενον ἐκ τοῦ Υἱοῦ, 77, 81

Macedonian Heresy, 77, 85, 145, 153
Macedonius (4th cent.), 85
────── (6th cent.), 8
Marcellus of Ancyra, 25, 54, 72, 85
Mary the Virgin, St., 104
Millenary the 6th, 123
Monothelete Controversy, 128
Mozarabic Breviary, 9

Nestorian Heresy, 48, 104, 147
Nestorius, 103
Nicolas I., Pope, 91
Nicolas, M., 3, 5
Newman—Arians of the 4th Century, 53 sqq.
────── notes to Oxford Translation of St. Athanasius, 53 sqq.
────── on the Nicene Anathema, 65
────── on the Character of Eusebius, 63
Novatians, 23

Origen, 160
Origin of the Creed, 5
Ommanney, Mr., on Athanasian Creed, 127
οἰκονομία, 111
ὁμοούσιος, 60, 70
Οὐσία, 60-64

Palmer, Sir W., 95
Patripassian Heresy, 28, 144
Paulinus, Patriarch of Aquileia, 116
Pearson, Bp., 70, 91, 115
Persona, 66, 151
Pilate, 33
Pius IV., P. Creed of, Contravenes the 7th Canon of Ephesus, and the Chalcedon Definition, 114
Phillpotts, Bp., his letter to Earl Grey, 149
Pothinus, 18
Procession of the Holy Spirit, 157
"Prophets who spake by the," 87
Psalters, Scribes of, encouraged by Charlemagne, 16
Pusey, Dr., on the Filioque, 88, 128
Πίστις, 8, 110
Πνευματόμαχοι, 85
Πρὶν γεννηθῆναι οὐκ ἦν, 65
Φύσεσι ἐν δύο, 113

Recared, 10, 88
Redditio Symboli, 12
Renunciations in Baptism, 49, 73, 96
Roman Creed long retained its original simplicity, 14
Rufinus, 3, 27

Sabellians, 144
Sozomen forbears to publish the Creed in his History, 55
Spirit, Personality of, acknowledged by Arians and Macedonians, 145
Swainson, Dr., 8, 16, 116
Swete, Dr., on the Procession, 90
Symbol, 6
Σύμβολον, 110
Σύνθεμα,

Tertullian, 22

Theodore, Archbishop of Canterbury, 126
Traditio Symboli, 12
Treves MS., 125
Θεολογία, 111
Θεοτόκος, 105, 128
Ταυτοούσιος, 65

Ussher, 5, 118
Utrecht MS., 118
—— Discovery of, 119
Ὑπόστασις in the Nicene Anathema, 65

Valentinian, 109
Vaughan, Dr., 150
Venantius Fortunatus, 122
Vienna MS., 120
Vincentius Lirinensis, 127, 130, 138
Vossius, 3, 7, 115

Waterland, 115 sqq.
Westwood, Professor, 119
Whiston, 72

By the same Author.

HARMONIA SYMBOLICA: A Collection of Creeds belonging to the Ancient Western Church and to the Mediæval English Church, arranged in Chronological order, and after the Manner of a Harmony. 8vo., cloth, price 6s. 6d.

OXFORD, AT THE CLARENDON PRESS.

PAROCHIAL SERMONS: Preached in a Village Church. Fourth Series. Price 5s. 6d.

RIVINGTONS: LONDON, OXFORD, AND CAMBRIDGE.

THE UNION BETWEEN CHRIST AND HIS PEOPLE: Four Sermons preached before the University of Oxford. Second Edition. 8vo., cloth, price 5s. 6d.

JUSTIFICATION: Eight Sermons preached before the University of Oxford, being the BAMPTON LECTURE for 1845. Second Edition. 8vo., cloth, price 9s.

AN INQUIRY INTO THE SCRIPTURAL WARRANT FOR ADDRESSING PRAYER TO CHRIST. Price 1s.

SERMONS ON SOME SUBJECTS OF RECENT CONTROVERSY, preached before the University of Oxford: I. The Scripture method of dealing with Questions relating to Outward Observances. II. The Eucharistic Sacrifice. III. The better Covenant. IV. The Shiloh. V. Summary View of the Christian Evidences. Price 5s.

THE FUTURE OF THE UNGODLY: ETERNAL LIFE, GOD'S GIFT IN CHRIST: Two Sermons preached before the University of Oxford, 1879. Price 1s.

THE ATHANASIAN CREED: Reasons for rejecting Mr. FFOULKES's Theory as to its Age and Author. Price 1s.

THE CHILDREN'S TEETH SET ON EDGE BY THE SOUR GRAPES EATEN BY THEIR FATHERS. A SERMON preached in Christ Church Cathedral on Sunday, Oct. 11, 1885, being the Sunday preceding the Bicentenary of the Revocation of the Edict of Nantes.

OXFORD AND LONDON: JAMES PARKER AND CO.

Uniform Works.

DE FIDE ET SYMBOLO: Documenta quædam nec non Aliquorum SS. Patrum Tractatus. Edidit CAROLUS A. HEURTLEY, S. T. P. Editio Tertia, Recognita et Aucta. Crown 8vo., cloth, 4s. 6d.

THE TEACHING OF THE TWELVE APOSTLES. Διδαχὴ τῶν δώδεκα Ἀποστόλων. The Greek Text with English Translation, Introduction, Notes, and Illustrative Passages. By the Rev. H. DE ROMESTIN, Incumbent of Freeland, and Rural Dean. Fcap. 8vo., cloth, 3s.

THE CANONS. The Definitions of the Catholic Faith and Canons of Discipline of the First Four General Councils of the Universal Church. In Greek and English. Fcap. 8vo., cloth, 2s. 6d.

S. AURELIUS AUGUSTINUS, EPISCOPUS HIPPONENSIS, De Catechizandis Rudibus, and other Treatises. The Edition as edited by the late CHARLES MARRIOTT, with the addition of the Enchiridion. Fourth Edition, Fcap. 8vo., cloth, 3s. 6d.

SAINT AUGUSTINE, on Instructing the Unlearned, concerning Faith of Things not Seen, on the Advantage of Believing, the Enchiridion to Laurentius, or concerning Faith, Hope, and Charity. Edited by Rev. H. DE ROMESTIN, M.A., Vicar of Stony Stratford. Fcap. 8vo., cloth, 3s. 6d.

VINCENTIUS LIRINENSIS FOR THE ANTIQUITY AND UNIVERSALITY OF THE CATHOLIC FAITH AGAINST THE PROFANE NOVELTIES OF ALL HERETICS. Latin and English. Fcap. 8vo., cloth, 3s.

THE PASTORAL RULE OF ST. GREGORY. Sancti Gregorii Papæ Regulæ Pastoralis Liber. With English Translation. By Rev. H. R. BRAMLEY, M.A. Fcap. 8vo., 6s.

OXFORD AND LONDON: JAMES PARKER AND CO.

A SELECTION FROM THE PUBLICATIONS OF
JAMES PARKER AND CO.
OXFORD, AND 6 SOUTHAMPTON-STREET, STRAND, LONDON.

Meditations on the Life of Christ.
By THOMAS A KEMPIS. Newly discovered and fully authenticated. Translated and Edited by the Ven. Archdeacon WRIGHT, M.A., and the Rev. S. KETTLEWELL, M.A. Second Edition. Fcap. 8vo., cloth, 6s.

Memorials of the Episcopate of John Fielder Mackarness, D.D.,
Bishop of Oxford from 1870 to 1888. By the Rev. CHARLES COLERIDGE MACKARNESS, M.A., Vicar of St. Martin's, Scarborough. Crown 8vo., cloth, 5s.

The Holy Communion.
Four Visitation Addresses, A.D. 1891. By JOHN WORDSWORTH, D.D., Bishop of Salisbury. 8vo., cloth, 5s.

History of the Church of England,
FOR SCHOOLS AND FAMILIES. By the Rev. A. H. HORE, M.A., Trinity College, Oxford. Crown 8vo., cloth, 552 pp., 5s.

A Historical Companion to Hymns Ancient and Modern;
Containing the Greek and Latin; the German, Italian, French, Danish and Welsh Hymns; the first lines of the English Hymns; the Names of all Authors and Translators; Notes and Dates. Edited by the Rev. ROBERT MAUDE MOORSOM, M.A., Trin. Coll., Cambridge, formerly Rector of Sadberge, County Durham. 24mo., cloth, 5s.

The Apology of Tertullian for the Christians.
Translated with Introduction, Analysis, and Appendix containing the Letters of Pliny and Trajan respecting the Christians. By T. HERBERT BINDLEY, M.A., Merton College, Oxford. Crown 8vo., cloth, 3s. 6d.

A Short History of Clent.
By JOHN AMPHLETT, M.A., S.C.L., Barrister-at-Law. Crown 8vo., cloth, 5s.

A Brief History of the English Church.
By ALFRED CECIL SMITH, M.A., Vicar of Summertown, Oxford. Fcap. 8vo., limp cloth, 2s. 6d.

The Seven Sayings from the Cross:
ADDRESSES by WILLIAM BRIGHT, D.D., Canon of Christ Church, Oxford. Fcap. 8vo., limp cloth, 1s. 6d.

Lays of the Early English Church.
By W. FOXLEY NORRIS, M.A., Rector of Witney. Fcap. 8vo., cloth, with Twelve Illustrations, 3s. 6d.

Lost Chords.
By W. MOORE, Rector of Appleton; late Fellow of Magdalen College, Oxford. Fcap. 8vo., cloth, 3s.

The One Religion.
Truth, Holiness, and Peace desired by the Nations, and Revealed by Jesus Christ. By the Right Rev. the LORD BISHOP OF SALISBURY. Second Edition. Crown 8vo., cloth, 7s. 6d.

The Administration of the Holy Spirit
IN THE BODY OF CHRIST. The Bampton Lectures for 1868. By the late LORD BISHOP OF SALISBURY. Third Edition. Crown 8vo., 7s. 6d.

An Explanation of the Thirty-Nine Articles.
By the late A. P. FORBES, D.C.L., Bishop of Brechin. With an Epistle Dedicatory to the Rev. E. B. PUSEY, D.D. New Edition, in one vol., Post 8vo., 12s.

A Short Explanation of the Nicene Creed,
For the Use of Persons beginning the Study of Theology. By the late A. P. FORBES, D.C.L., Bishop of Brechin. New Edition, Crown 8vo., cloth, 6s.

The Apostles' Creed.
The Greek Origin of the Apostles' Creed Illustrated by Ancient Documents and Recent Research. By Rev. JOHN BARON, D.D., F.S.A. 8vo., cloth, with Seven Illustrations, 10s. 6d.

The History of Confirmation.
By WILLIAM JACKSON, M.A., Queen's College, Oxford; Vicar of Heathfield, Sussex. Crown 8vo., cloth, 2s. 6d.

A Summary of the Ecclesiastical Courts Commission's Report:
And of Dr. STUBBS' Historical Reports; together with a Review of the Evidence before the Commission. By SPENCER L. HOLLAND, Barrister-at-Law. Post 8vo., cloth, 7s. 6d.

A History of Canon Law
In conjunction with other Branches of Jurisprudence: with Chapters on the Royal Supremacy and the Report of the Commission on Ecclesiastical Courts. By Rev. J. DODD, M.A., formerly Rector of Hampton Poyle, Oxon. 8vo., cloth, 7s. 6d.

On Eucharistical Adoration.

With Considerations suggested by a Pastoral Letter on the Doctrine of the Most Holy Eucharist. By the late Rev. JOHN KEBLE, M.A., Vicar of Hursley. 24mo., sewed, 2s.

The Catholic Doctrine of the Sacrifice and Participation of the Holy Eucharist.

By GEORGE TREVOR, M.A., D.D., Canon of York; Rector of Beeford. Second Edition. 8vo., cloth, 10s. 6d.

S. Athanasius on the Incarnation, &c.

S. Patris Nostri S. Athanasii Archiepiscopi Alexandriæ de Incarnatione Verbi, ejusque Corporali ad nos Adventu. With an English Translation by the Rev. J. RIDGWAY, B.D., Hon. Canon of Ch. Ch. Fcap. 8vo., cloth, 5s.

De Fide et Symbolo:

Documenta quædam nec non Aliquorum SS. Patrum Tractatus. Edidit CAROLUS A. HEURTLEY, S.T.P., Dom. Margaretæ Prælector, et Ædis Christi Canonicus. Editio Quarta, Recognita et Aucta. Crown 8vo., cloth, 4s. 6d.

Translation of the above.
Cloth, 4s. 6d.

The Canons of the Church.

The Definitions of the Catholic Faith and Canons of Discipline of the First Four General Councils of the Universal Church. In Greek and English. Fcap. 8vo., cloth, 2s. 6d.

The English Canons.

The Constitutions and Canons Ecclesiastical of the Church of England, referred to their Original Sources, and Illustrated with Explanatory Notes, by MACKENZIE E. C. WALCOTT, B.D., F.S.A., Præcentor and Prebendary of Chichester. Fcap. 8vo., cloth, 2s. 6d.

St. Cyril on the Mysteries.

The Five Lectures of St. Cyril on the Mysteries, and other Sacramental Treatises; with Translations. Edited by the Rev. H. DE ROMESTIN, M.A., Great Maplestead, Essex. Fcap. 8vo., cloth, 3s.

S. Aurelius Augustinus,

EPISCOPUS HIPPONENSIS,

De Catechizandis Rudibus, de Fide Rerum quæ non videntur, de Utilitate Credendi. A New Edition, with the Enchiridion. Fcap. 8vo., cloth, 3s. 6d.

Translation of the above.
Cloth, 3s. 6d.

Vincentius Lirinensis.

For the Antiquity and Universality of the Catholic Faith against the Profane Novelties of all Heretics. *Latin and English.* New Edition, Fcap. 8vo., 3s.

The Pastoral Rule of S. Gregory.

Sancti Gregorii Papæ Regulæ Pastoralis Liber, ad JOHANNEM, Episcopum Civitatis Ravennæ. With an English Translation. By the Rev. H. R. BRAMLEY, M.A., Fellow of Magdalen College, Oxford. Fcap. 8vo., cloth, 6s.

The Athanasian Creed.

A Critical History of the Athanasian Creed, by the Rev. DANIEL WATERLAND, D.D. Fcap. 8vo., cloth, 5s.

Διδαχὴ τῶν δώδεκα Ἀποστόλων.

The Teaching of the Twelve Apostles. The Greek Text with English Translation, Introduction, Notes, and Illustrative Passages. By the Rev. H. DE ROMESTIN, Incumbent of Freeland, and Rural Dean. Second Edition. Fcap. 8vo., cloth, 3s.

Studia Sacra:

Commentaries on the Introductory Verses of St. John's Gospel, and on a Portion of St. Paul's Epistle to the Romans; with an Analysis of St. Paul's Epistles, &c., by the late Rev. JOHN KEBLE, M.A. 8vo., cloth, 10s. 6d.

Discourses on Prophecy.

In which are considered its Structure, Use and Inspiration. By JOHN DAVISON, B.D. Sixth and Cheaper Edition. 8vo., cloth, 9s.

The Worship of the Old Covenant

CONSIDERED MORE ESPECIALLY IN RELATION TO THAT OF THE New. By the Rev. E. F. WILLIS, M.A., late Vice-Principal of Cuddesdon College. Post 8vo., cloth, 5s.

A Summary of the Evidences for the Bible.

By the Rev. T. S. ACKLAND, M.A., late Fellow of Clare Hall, Cambridge; Incumbent of Pollington cum Balne, Yorkshire. 24mo., cloth, 3s.

A Plain Commentary on the Book of Psalms

(Prayer-book Version), chiefly grounded on the Fathers. For the Use of Families. 2 vols., Fcap. 8vo., cloth, 10s. 6d.

The Psalter and the Gospel.

The Life, Sufferings, and Triumph of our Blessed Lord, revealed in the Book of Psalms. Fcap. 8vo., cloth, 2s.

The Study of the New Testament:

Its Present Position, and some of its Problems. AN INAUGURAL LECTURE delivered on Feb. 20th and 22nd, 1883. By W. SANDAY, M.A., D.D., Dean Ireland's Professor of the Exegesis of Holy Scripture. 64 pp. 8vo., in wrapper, 2s.

Sayings Ascribed to Our Lord

By the Fathers and other Primitive Writers, and Incidents in His Life narrated by them, otherwise than found in Scripture. By JOHN THEODORE DODD, B.A., late Student of Christ Church, Oxford. Fcap. 8vo., cloth, 3s.

A Commentary on the Epistles and Gospels in the Book of Common Prayer.

Extracted from Writings of the Fathers of the Holy Catholic Church, anterior to the Division of the East and West. With an Introductory Notice by the DEAN OF ST. PAUL'S. 2 vols., Crown 8vo., cloth, 10s. 6d.

Catena Aurea.

A Commentary on the Four Gospels, collected out of the Works of the Fathers by S. THOMAS AQUINAS. Uniform with the Library of the Fathers. A Re-issue, complete in 6 vols., cloth, £2 2s.

A Plain Commentary on the Four Holy Gospels,

Intended chiefly for Devotional Reading. By the Very Rev. J. W. BURGON, B.D., Dean of Chichester. New Edition. 4 vols., Fcap. 8vo., limp cloth, £1 1s.

The Last Twelve Verses of the Gospel according to S. Mark

Vindicated against Recent Critical Objectors and Established, by the Very Rev. J. W. BURGON, B.D., Dean of Chichester. With Facsimiles of Codex א and Codex L. 8vo., cloth, 6s.

The Gospels from a Rabbinical Point of View,

Shewing the perfect Harmony of the Four Evangelists on the subject of our Lord's Last Supper, and the Bearing of the Laws and Customs of the Jews at the time of our Lord's coming on the Language of the Gospels. By the late Rev. G. W. PIERITZ, M.A. Crown 8vo., limp cloth, 3s.

Christianity as Taught by S. Paul.

By the late W. J. IRONS, D.D., of Queen's College, Oxford; Prebendary of S. Paul's; being the BAMPTON LECTURES for the Year 1870, with an Appendix of the CONTINUOUS SENSE of S. Paul's Epistles; with Notes and Metalegomena, 8vo., with Map, Second Edition, with New Preface, cloth, 9s.

S. Paul's Epistles to the Ephesians and Philippians.

A Practical and Exegetical Commentary. Edited by the late Rev. HENRY NEWLAND. 8vo., cloth, 7s. 6d.

The Explanation of the Apocalypse.

By VENERABLE BEDA, Translated by the Rev. EDW. MARSHALL, M.A., F.S.A., formerly Fellow of Corpus Christi College, Oxford. 180 pp. Fcap. 8vo., cloth, 3s. 6d.

A History of the Church,
From the Edict of Milan, A.D. 313, to the Council of Chalcedon, A.D. 451. By WILLIAM BRIGHT, D.D., Regius Professor of Ecclesiastical History, and Canon of Christ Church, Oxford. Second Edition. Post 8vo., 10s. 6d.

The Age of the Martyrs;
Or, The First Three Centuries of the Work of the Church of our Lord and Saviour Jesus Christ. By the late JOHN DAVID JENKINS, B.D., Fellow of Jesus College, Oxford; Canon of Pieter Maritzburg. Cr. 8vo., cl., reduced to 3s. 6d.

The Church in England from William III. to Victoria.
By the Rev. A. H. HORE, M.A., Trinity College, Oxford. 2 vols., Post 8vo., cloth, 15s.

The Ecclesiastical History of the First Three Centuries,
From the Crucifixion of Jesus Christ to the year 313. By the late Rev. Dr. BURTON. Fourth Edition. 8vo., cloth, 12s.

A Brief History of the Christian Church,
From the First Century to the Reformation. By the Rev. J. S. BARTLETT. Fcap. 8vo., cloth, 2s. 6d.

A History of the English Church,
From its Foundation to the Reign of Queen Mary. By MARY CHARLOTTE STAPLEY. Fourth Edition, revised, with a Recommendatory Notice by DEAN HOOK. Crown 8vo., cloth, 5s.

Bede's Ecclesiastical History of the English Nation.
A New Translation by the Rev. L. GIDLEY, M.A., Chaplain of St. Nicholas', Salisbury. Crown 8vo., cloth, 6s.

St. Paul in Britain;
Or, The Origin of British as opposed to Papal Christianity. By the Rev. R. W. MORGAN. Second Edition. Crown 8vo., cloth, 2s. 6d.

The Sufferings of the Clergy during the Great Rebellion.
By the Rev. JOHN WALKER, M.A., sometime of Exeter College, Oxford, and Rector of St. Mary Major, Exeter. Epitomised by the Author of "The Annals of England." Second Edition. Fcap. 8vo., cloth, 2s. 6d.

Missale ad usum Insignis et Præclaræ Ecclesiæ Sarum

Ed. F. H. DICKINSON, A.M. Complete in One Vol., 8vo., cl., 26s. Part II., 6s.; Part III., 10s. 6d.; and Part IV., 7s. 6d.; may still be had.

The First Prayer-Book of Edward VI. Compared

With the Successive Revisions of the Book of Common Prayer. Together with a Concordance and Index to the Rubrics in the several Editions. Second Edition. Crown 8vo., cloth, 12s.

An Introduction

TO THE HISTORY OF THE SUCCESSIVE REVIsions of the Book of Common Prayer. By JAMES PARKER, Hon. M.A. Oxon. Crown 8vo., pp. xxxii., 532, cloth, 12s.

The Principles of Divine Service

Or, An Inquiry concerning the True Manner of Understanding and Using the Order for Morning and Evening Prayer, and for the Administration of the Holy Communion in the English Church. By the late Ven. PHILIP FREEMAN, M.A., Archdeacon of Exeter, &c. 2 vols., 8vo., cloth, 16s.

A History of the Book of Common Prayer,

And other Authorized Books, from the Reformation; with an Account of the State of Religion in England from 1640 to 1660. By the Rev. THOMAS LATHBURY, M.A. Second Edition, with an Index. 8vo., cloth, 5s.

The Prayer-Book Calendar.

THE CALENDAR OF THE PRAYER-BOOK ILLUSTRATED. (Comprising the first portion of the "Calendar of the Anglican Church," with additional Illustrations, an Appendix on Emblems, &c.) With 200 Engravings from Medieval Works of Art. Sixth Thousand. Fcap. 8vo., cl., 6s.

A CHEAP EDITION OF

The First Prayer-Book

As issued by the Authority of the Parliament of the Second Year of King Edward VI. 1549. Tenth Thousand. 24mo., limp cloth, price 1s.

Also,

The Second Prayer-Book of Edward VI.

Issued 1552. Fifth Thousand. 24mo., limp cloth, price 1s.

Ritual Conformity.

Interpretations of the Rubrics of the Prayer-Book, agreed upon by a Conference held at All Saints, Margaret-street, 1880—1881. Third Edition, 80 pp. Crown 8vo., in wrapper, 1s.

The Ornaments Rubrick,

ITS HISTORY AND MEANING. Fifth Thousand. 72 pp., Crown 8vo., 6d.

The Catechist's Manual;

By EDW. M. HOLMES, Rector of Marsh Gibbon, Bicester. With an Introduction by the late SAMUEL WILBERFORCE, LORD BP. OF WINCHESTER. 6th Thousand. Cr. 8vo., limp cl., 5s.

The Confirmation Class-book:

Notes for Lessons, with APPENDIX, containing Questions and Summaries for the Use of the Candidates. By EDWARD M. HOLMES, LL.B., Author of the "Catechist's Manual." Second Edition, Fcap. 8vo., limp cloth, 2s. 6d.

THE QUESTIONS, separate, 4 sets, in wrapper, 1s.
THE SUMMARIES, separate, 4 sets, in wrapper, 1s.

Catechetical Lessons on the Book of Common Prayer.

Illustrating the Prayer-book, from its Title-page to the end of the Collects, Epistles, and Gospels. Designed to aid the Clergy in Public Catechising. By the Rev. Dr. FRANCIS HESSEY, Incumbent of St. Barnabas, Kensington. Fcap. 8vo., cloth, 6s.

Catechising Notes on the Apostles' Creed;

The Ten Commandments; The Lord's Prayer; The Confirmation Service; The Forms of Prayer at Sea, &c. By A WORCESTERSHIRE CURATE. Crown 8vo., in wrapper, 1s.

The Church's Work in our Large Towns.

By GEORGE HUNTINGTON, M.A., Rector of Tenby, and Domestic Chaplain of the Rt. Hon. the Earl of Crawford and Balcarres. Second Edit., revised and enlarged. Cr. 8vo., cl. 3s. 6d.

Notes of Seven Years' Work in a Country Parish.

By R. F. WILSON, M.A., Prebendary of Sarum, and Examining Chaplain to the Bishop of Salisbury. Fcap. 8vo., cloth, 4s.

A Manual of Pastoral Visitation,

Intended for the Use of the Clergy in their Visitation of the Sick and Afflicted. By A PARISH PRIEST. Dedicated, by permission, to His Grace the Archbishop of Dublin. Second Edition, Crown 8vo., limp cloth, 3s. 6d.; roan, 4s.

The Cure of Souls.

By the Rev. G. ARDEN, M.A., Rector of Winterborne-Came, and Author of "Breviates from Holy Scripture," &c. Fcap. 8vo., cloth, 2s. 6d.

Questions on the Collects, Epistles, and Gospels,

Throughout the Year. Edited by the Rev. T. L. CLAUGHTON, Vicar of Kidderminster. For the Use of Teachers in Sunday Schools. Fifth Edition, 18mo., cl. In two Parts, each 2s. 6d.

Addresses to the Candidates for Ordination on the Questions in the Ordination Service.

By the late SAMUEL WILBERFORCE, LORD BISHOP OF WINCHESTER. Fifth Thousand. Crown 8vo., cloth, 6s.

Tracts for the Christian Seasons.

FIRST SERIES. Edited by JOHN ARMSTRONG, D.D., late Lord Bishop of Grahamstown. 4 vols. complete, Fcap. 8vo., cloth, 12s.

SECOND SERIES. Edited by JOHN ARMSTRONG, D.D., late Lord Bishop of Grahamstown. 4 vols. complete, Fcap. 8vo., cloth, 10s.

THIRD SERIES. Edited by JAMES RUSSELL WOODFORD, D.D., late Lord Bishop of Ely. 4 vols., Fcap. 8vo., cloth, 14s.

Faber's Stories from the Old Testament.

With Four Illustrations. New Edition. Square Crown 8vo., cloth, 4s.

Holy Order.

A CATECHISM. By CHARLES S. GRUEBER, Vicar of S. James, Hambridge, Diocese of Bath and Wells. 220 pp. 24mo., in wrapper, 3s.

By the same Author.

The Church of England the Ancient Church of the Land.

Its Property. Disestablishment and Disendowment. Fate of Sacrilege. Work and Progress of the Church, &c., &c. A CATECHISM. Fourth thousand, 24mo., limp cloth, 1s.

A Catechism on the Church, The Kingdom of God:

For the Use of the Children of the Kingdom. Fourth thousand, 280 pp. 24mo., limp cloth, 2s.

"Is Christ Divided?"

On Unity in Religion, and the Sin and Scandal of Schism, That is to say, of Division, Disunion, Separation, among Christians. A CATECHISM. 8vo., in wrapper, 1s.

The Catechism of the Church of England

Commented upon, and Illustrated from the Holy Scriptures and the Book of Common Prayer, with Appendices on Confirmation, &c., &c. Third thousand, 24mo., limp cloth, 1s.

For a Series of Parochial Books and Tracts published by Messrs. Parker, see the Parochial Catalogue.

Oxford Editions of Devotional Works.

Fcap. 8vo., chiefly printed in Red and Black, on Toned Paper. Also kept in a variety of Leather Bindings.

Andrewes' Devotions.
DEVOTIONS. By the Right Rev. Lancelot Andrewes. Translated from the Greek and Latin, and arranged anew. Cloth, 5s.

The Imitation of Christ.
FOUR BOOKS. By Thomas à Kempis. A new Edition, revised. Cloth, 4s.
Pocket Edition. 32mo., cloth, 1s.; bound, 1s. 6d.

Laud's Devotions.
THE PRIVATE DEVOTIONS of Dr. William Laud, Archbishop of Canterbury, and Martyr. Antique cloth, 5s.

Spinckes' Devotions.
TRUE CHURCH OF ENGLAND MAN'S COMPANION IN THE CLOSET. By Nathaniel Spinckes. Floriated borders, antique cloth, 4s.

Sutton's Meditations.
GODLY MEDITATIONS UPON THE MOST HOLY SACRAMENT OF THE LORD'S SUPPER. By Christopher Sutton, D.D., late Prebend of Westminster. A new Edition. Antique cloth, 5s.

Devout Communicant.
THE DEVOUT COMMUNICANT, exemplified in his Behaviour before, at, and after the Sacrament of the Lord's Supper: Practically suited to all the Parts of that Solemn Ordinance. 7th Edition, revised. Edited by Rev. G. Moultrie. Fcap. 8vo., toned paper, red lines, ant. cloth, 4s.

Taylor's Holy Living.
THE RULE AND EXERCISES OF HOLY LIVING. By Bishop Jeremy Taylor. Antique cloth, 4s.
Pocket Edition. 32mo., cloth, 1s. bound, 1s. 6d.

Taylor's Holy Dying.
THE RULE AND EXERCISES OF HOLY DYING. By Bishop Jeremy Taylor. Ant. cloth, 4s.
Pocket Edition. 32mo., cloth, 1s.; bound, 1s. 6d.

Taylor's Golden Grove.
THE GOLDEN GROVE: A Choice Manual, containing what is to be Believed, Practised, and Desired or Prayed for. By Bishop Jeremy Taylor. Antique cloth, 3s. 6d.

Wilson's Sacra Privata.
SACRA PRIVATA. The Private Meditations, Devotions, and Prayers of the Right Rev. T. Wilson, D.D., Lord Bishop of Sodor and Man. Now first Printed entire, from the Original Manuscripts. Antique cloth, 4s.

ΕΙΚΩΝ ΒΑΣΙΛΙΚΗ.
THE PORTRAITURE OF HIS SACRED MAJESTY KING CHARLES I. in his Solitudes and Sufferings. New Edition, with an Historical Preface by C. M. Phillimore. Cloth, 5s.

Ancient Collects.
ANCIENT COLLECTS AND OTHER PRAYERS, Selected for Devotional Use from various Rituals, with an Appendix on the Collects in the Prayer-book. By William Bright, D.D. Fourth Edition. Antique cloth, 5s.

EUCHARISTICA:
Meditations and Prayers on the Most Holy Eucharist, from Old English Divines. With an Introduction by SAMUEL, LORD BISHOP OF OXFORD. A New Edition, revised by the Rev. H. E. CLAYTON, Vicar of S. Mary Magdalene, Oxford. In Red and Black, 32mo., cloth, 2s. 6d.—Cheap Edition, 1s.

DAILY STEPS TOWARDS HEAVEN;
Or, PRACTICAL THOUGHTS on the GOSPEL HISTORY, for Every Day in the Year. 50th Thous. 32mo., roan, 2s. 6d.; mor., 5s.
LARGE-TYPE EDITION. Crown 8vo., cloth antique, 5s.

THE HOURS:
Being Prayers for the Third, Sixth, and Ninth Hours; with a Preface and Heads of Devotion for the Day. Seventh Edition. 32mo., 1s.

PRIVATE PRAYERS FOR A WEEK.
Compiled by WILLIAM BRIGHT, D.D., Canon of Christ Church, Oxford. 96 pp. Fcap. 8vo., limp cloth, 1s. 6d.

By the same Author.

FAMILY PRAYERS FOR A WEEK.
Fcap. 8vo., cloth, 1s.

STRAY THOUGHTS:
For Every Day in the Year. Collected and Arranged by E. L. 32mo., cloth gilt, red edges, 1s.

OUTLINES OF INSTRUCTIONS
Or Meditations for the Church's Seasons. By the late JOHN KEBLE, M.A. Edited, with a Preface, by the late R. F. WILSON, M.A. 2nd Edition. Cr. 8vo., cloth, toned paper, 5s.

SPIRITUAL COUNSEL, ETC.
By the late Rev. J. KEBLE, M.A. Edited by the late R. F. WILSON, M.A. Fifth Edition. Post 8vo., cloth, 3s. 6d.

MEDITATIONS FOR THE FORTY DAYS OF LENT.
By the Author of "Charles Lowder." With a Prefatory Notice by the ARCHBISHOP OF DUBLIN. 18mo., cloth, 2s. 6d.

OF THE IMITATION OF CHRIST.
Four Books. By THOMAS A KEMPIS. Small 4to., printed on thick toned paper, with red border-lines, &c. Cloth, 12s.

PRAYERS FOR MARRIED PERSONS.
From Various Sources, chiefly from the Ancient Liturgies. Selected by C. WARD, M.A. Third Edition, Revised. 24mo., cloth, 4s. 6d.; Cheap Edition, 2s. 6d.

FOR THE LORD'S SUPPER.
DEVOTIONS BEFORE AND AFTER HOLY COMMUNION. With Preface by J. KEBLE. Sixth Edition. 32mo., cloth, 2s. With the Office, cloth, 2s. 6d.

A MENOLOGY;
Or Record of Departed Friends. 16mo., cloth, 3s.

The late Osborne Gordon.

OSBORNE GORDON. A Memoir: with a Selection of his Writings. Edited by GEO. MARSHALL, M.A., Rector of Milton, Berks, &c. With Medallion Portrait, 8vo., cloth, 10s. 6d.

Dr. Preston.

THE LIFE OF THE RENOWNED DR. PRESTON. Writ by his Pupil, Master THOMAS BALL, D.D., Minister of Northampton in the year 1628. Edited by E. W. HARCOURT, Esq., M.P. Crown 8vo., cloth, 4s.

Rev. John Keble.

A MEMOIR OF THE REV. JOHN KEBLE, M.A., late Vicar of Hursley. By the Right Hon. Sir J. T. COLERIDGE, D.C.L. Fifth Edition. Post 8vo., cloth, 6s.

OCCASIONAL PAPERS AND REVIEWS, on Sir Walter Scott, Poetry, and Sacred Poetry. By the late Rev. JOHN KEBLE. Author of "The Christian Year." Demy 8vo., cloth extra, 12s.

Archdeacon Denison.

NOTES OF MY LIFE, 1805—1878. By GEORGE ANTHONY DENISON, Vicar of East Brent, 1845: Archdeacon of Taunton, 1851. Third Edition, 8vo., cloth, 12s.

Bishop Herbert de Losinga.

THE FOUNDER OF NORWICH CATHEDRAL. The LIFE, LETTERS, and SERMONS of BISHOP HERBERT DE LOSINGA (b. circ. A.D. 1050, d. 1119). By EDWARD MEYRICK GOULBURN, D.D., Dean of Norwich, and HENRY SYMONDS, M.A. 2 vols., 8vo., cloth, 30s.

John Armstrong.

LIFE OF JOHN ARMSTRONG, D.D., late Lord Bishop of Grahamstown. By the Rev. T. T. CARTER, M.A., Rector of Clewer. Third Edition. Fcap. 8vo., with Portrait, cloth, 7s. 6d.

Bishop Wilson.

THE LIFE OF THE RIGHT REVEREND FATHER IN GOD, THOMAS WILSON, D.D., Lord Bishop of Sodor and Man. By the late Rev. JOHN KEBLE, M.A., Vicar of Hursley. 2 vols. 8vo., cloth, £1 1s.

THE SAINTLY LIFE OF MRS. MARGARET GODOLPHIN. 16mo., 1s.

FOOTPRINTS ON THE SANDS OF TIME. BIOGRAPHIES FOR YOUNG PEOPLE. Fcap., limp cloth, 2s. 6d.

THE AUTHORIZED EDITIONS OF
THE CHRISTIAN YEAR,
With the Author's latest Corrections and Additions.

NOTICE.—Messrs. PARKER are the sole Publishers of the Editions of the "Christian Year" issued with the sanction and under the direction of the Author's representatives. All Editions without their imprint are unauthorized.

	s.	d.		s.	d.
Handsomely printed on toned paper. SMALL 4to. EDITION.			32mo. EDITION.		
Cloth extra . . .	10	6	Cloth, limp	1	0
			Cloth boards, gilt edges .	1	6
DEMY 8vo. EDITION. Cloth	6	0	48mo. EDITION.		
			Cloth, limp	0	6
FCAP. 8vo. EDITION. Cloth	3	6	Roan	1	6
24mo. EDIT. With red lines, cl.	2	6	FACSIMILE OF THE 1ST EDITION. 2 vols., 12mo., boards	7	6

The above Editions are kept in a variety of bindings.

By the same Author.

LYRA INNOCENTIUM. Thoughts in Verse on Christian Children. *Thirteenth Edition.* Fcap. 8vo., cloth, 5s.
——————— 48mo. edition, limp cloth, 6d.; cloth boards, 1s.
MISCELLANEOUS POEMS by the Rev. JOHN KEBLE, M.A., Vicar of Hursley. *Third Edition.* Fcap. cloth, 6s.
THE PSALTER OR PSALMS OF DAVID: In English Verse. *Fourth Edition.* Fcap., cloth, 6s.

The above may also be had in various bindings.

By the late Rev. ISAAC WILLIAMS.

THE CATHEDRAL; or, The Catholic and Apostolic Church in England. Fcap. 8vo., cloth, 5s.; 32mo., cloth, 2s. 6d.
THE BAPTISTERY; or, The Way of Eternal Life. Fcap. 8vo., cloth, 7s. 6d. (with the Plates); 32mo., cloth, 2s. 6d.
HYMNS translated from the PARISIAN BREVIARY. 32mo., cloth, 2s. 6d.
THE CHRISTIAN SCHOLAR. Fcap. 8vo., cloth, 5s.; 32mo., cloth, 2s. 6d.
THOUGHTS IN PAST YEARS. 32mo., cloth, 2s. 6d.
THE SEVEN DAYS; or, The Old and New Creation. Fcap. 8vo., cloth, 3s. 6d.

CHRISTIAN BALLADS AND POEMS.

By ARTHUR CLEVELAND COXE, D.D., Bishop of Western New York. A New Edition, printed in Red and Black, Fcap. 8vo., cloth, 2s. 6d.—Cheap Edition, 1s.

The POEMS of GEORGE HERBERT.

THE TEMPLE. Sacred Poems and Private Ejaculations. A New Edition, in Red and Black, 24mo., cloth, 2s. 6d.—Cheap Edition, 1s.

THE ARCHBISHOP OF CANTERBURY.

SINGLEHEART. By Dr. EDWARD WHITE BENSON, Archbishop of Canterbury, late Bishop of Truro, &c. ADVENT SERMONS, 1876, preached in Lincoln Cathedral. Second Edition. Crown 8vo., cloth, 2s. 6d.

THE BISHOP OF SALISBURY.

UNIVERSITY SERMONS ON GOSPEL SUBJECTS. By the Right Rev. the LORD BISHOP OF SALISBURY. Fcap. 8vo., cl., 2s. 6d.

THE LATE BISHOP OF SALISBURY.

SERMONS ON THE BEATITUDES, with others mostly preached before the University of Oxford; to which is added a Preface relating to the volume of "Essays and Reviews." New Edition. Crown 8vo., cloth, 7s. 6d.

THE BISHOP OF NEWCASTLE.

THE AWAKING SOUL. As sketched in the 130th Psalm. Addresses delivered at St. Peter's, Eaton-square, on the Tuesdays in Lent, 1877, by E. R. WILBERFORCE, M.A. [Rt. Rev. the Lord Bp. of Newcastle]. Crown 8vo., limp cloth, 2s. 6d.

THE BISHOP OF BARBADOS.

SERMONS PREACHED ON SPECIAL OCCASIONS. By JOHN MITCHINSON, D.D., late Bishop of Barbados. Crown 8vo., cloth, 5s.

VERY REV. THE DEAN OF CHICHESTER.

SHORT SERMONS FOR FAMILY READING, following the Course of the Christian Seasons. By Very Rev. J. W. BURGON, B.D., Dean of Chichester. First Series. 2 vols., Fcap. 8vo., cloth, 8s.
——— SECOND SERIES. 2 vols., Fcap. 8vo., cloth, 8s.

VERY REV. THE DEAN OF ROCHESTER.

HINTS TO PREACHERS, ILLUSTRATED BY SERMONS AND ADDRESSES. By S. REYNOLDS HOLE, Dean of Rochester. Second Edition. Post 8vo., cloth, 6s.

REV. J. KEBLE.

SERMONS, OCCASIONAL AND PAROCHIAL. By the late Rev. JOHN KEBLE, M.A., Vicar of Hursley. 8vo., cloth, 12s.

THE REV. CANON PAGET.

THE REDEMPTION OF WORK. ADDRESSES spoken in St. Paul's Cathedral, by FRANCIS PAGET, M.A., Senior Student of Christ Church, Oxford. 52 pp. Fcap. 8vo., cloth, 2s.

CONCERNING SPIRITUAL GIFTS. Three Addresses to Candidates for Holy Orders in the Diocese of Ely. With a Sermon. By FRANCIS PAGET, M.A., Senior Student of Christ Church, Oxford. Fcap. 8vo., cloth, 2s. 6d.

Works of the Standard English Divines,
PUBLISHED IN THE LIBRARY OF ANGLO-CATHOLIC THEOLOGY.

Andrewes' (Bp.) Complete Works. 11 vols., 8vo., £3 7s.
    The Sermons. (Separate.) 5 vols., £1 15s.

Beveridge's (Bp.) Complete Works. 12 vols., 8vo., £4 4s.
    The English Theological Works. 10 vols., £3 10s.

Bramhall's (Abp.) Works, with Life and Letters, &c. 5 vols., 8vo., £1 15s.

Bull's (Bp.) Harmony on Justification. 2 vols., 8vo., 10s.
————— **Defence of the Nicene Creed.** 2 vols., 10s.
————— **Judgment of the Catholic Church.** 5s.

Cosin's (Bp.) Works Complete. 5 vols., 8vo., £1 10s.

Crakanthorp's Defensio Ecclesiæ Anglicanæ. 8vo., 7s.

Frank's Sermons. 2 vols., 8vo., 10s.

Forbes' Considerationes Modestæ. 2 vols., 8vo., 12s.

Gunning's Paschal, or Lent Fast. 8vo., 6s.

Hammond's Practical Catechism. 8vo., 5s.
————— **Miscellaneous Theological Works.** 5s.
————— **Thirty-one Sermons.** 2 Parts. 10s.

Hickes's Two Treatises on the Christian Priesthood. 3 vols., 8vo., 15s.

Johnson's (John) Theological Works. 2 vols., 8vo., 10s.
————— **English Canons.** 2 vols., 12s.

Laud's (Abp.) Complete Works. 7 vols., (9 Parts,) 8vo., £2 17s.

L'Estrange's Alliance of Divine Offices. 8vo., 6s.

Marshall's Penitential Discipline. 8vo., 4s.

Nicholson's (Bp.) Exposition of the Catechism. (This volume cannot be sold separate from the complete set.)

Overall's (Bp.) Convocation-book of 1606. 8vo., 5s.

Pearson's (Bp.) Vindiciæ Epistolarum S. Ignatii. 2 vols., 8vo., 10s.

Thorndike's (Herbert) Theological Works Complete. 6 vols., (10 Parts,) 8vo., £2 10s.

Wilson's (Bp.) Works Complete. With Life, by Rev. J. Keble. 7 vols., (8 Parts,) 8vo., £3 3s.

    *** *The* 81 *Vols. in* 88, *for* £15 15s. *net.*

HISTORICAL TALES,

Illustrating the Chief Events in Ecclesiastical History British and Foreign, &c.

Fcap. 8vo., 1s. each Tale, or 3s. 6d. each Volume in cloth.

ENGLAND. Vol. I.

1.—THE CAVE IN THE HILLS; or, Cæcilius Viriathus.
5.—WILD SCENES AMONGST THE CELTS.
7.—THE RIVALS: A Tale of the Anglo-Saxon Church.
10.—THE BLACK DANES.
14.—THE ALLELUIA BATTLE; or, Pelagianism in Britain.

ENGLAND. Vol. II.

16.—ALICE OF FOBBING; or, The Times of Jack Straw and Wat Tyler.
18.—AUBREY DE L'ORNE; or, The Times of St. Anselm.
21.—THE FORSAKEN; or, The Times of St. Dunstan.
24.—WALTER THE ARMOURER; or, The Interdict.
27.—AGNES MARTIN; or, The Fall of Cardinal Wolsey.

AMERICA AND OUR COLONIES.

3.—THE CHIEF'S DAUGHTER; or, The Settlers in Virginia.
8.—THE CONVERT OF MASSACHUSETTS.
20.—WOLFINGHAM; or, The Convict Settler of Jervis Bay.
25.—THE CATECHUMENS OF THE COROMANDEL COAST.
28.—ROSE AND MINNIE; or, The Loyalist: A Tale of Canada in 1837.

FRANCE AND SPAIN.

2.—THE EXILES OF THE CEBENNA; a Journal written during the Decian Persecution.
22.—THE DOVE OF TABENNA; and THE RESCUE.
23.—LARACHE: A Tale of the Portuguese Church in the Sixteenth Century.
29.—DORES DE GUALDIM: A Tale of the Portuguese Revolution.

EASTERN AND NORTHERN EUROPE.

6.—THE LAZAR-HOUSE OF LEROS: a Tale of the Eastern Church.
11.—THE CONVERSION OF ST. VLADIMIR; or, The Martyrs of Kief.
13.—THE CROSS IN SWEDEN; or, The Days of King Ingi the Good.
17.—THE NORTHERN LIGHT: A Tale of Iceland and Greenland.
26.—THE DAUGHTERS OF POLA; a Tale of the Great Tenth Persecution.

ASIA AND AFRICA.

4.—THE LILY OF TIFLIS: a Sketch from Georgian Church History.
9.—THE QUAY OF THE DIOSCURI: a Tale of Nicene Times.
12.—THE SEA-TIGERS: A Tale of Mediæval Nestorianism.
15.—THE BRIDE OF RAMCUTTAH: A Tale of the Jewish Missions.
19.—LUCIA'S MARRIAGE; or, The Lions of Wady-Araba.

The late Dr. Elvey's Psalter.

Just published, 16mo., cloth, 1s.; by Post, 1s. 2d.

A CHEAP EDITION (being the 20th) of
THE PSALTER; or, Canticles and Psalms of David.
Pointed for Chanting on a New Principle. With Explanations and Directions. By the late STEPHEN ELVEY, Mus. Doc., Organist of New and St. John's Colleges, and Organist and Choragus to the University of Oxford. With a Memorandum on the Pointing of the *Gloria Patri*, by Sir G. J. ELVEY.

Also,

II. FCAP. 8vo. EDITION (the 21st), limp cloth, 2s. 6d. With PROPER PSALMS. 3s.
III. LARGE TYPE EDITION for ORGAN (the 18th). Demy 8vo., cloth, 5s.
THE PROPER PSALMS separately. Fcap. 8vo. sewed, 6d.
THE CANTICLES separately (18th Edition). Fcap. 8vo., 3d.

The Psalter is used at St. George's Chapel, Windsor, and at many Cathedrals.

OXFORD AND LONDON: JAMES PARKER AND CO.

www.ingramcontent.com/pod-product-compliance
Lightning Source LLC
Chambersburg PA
CBHW020240170426
43202CB00008B/155